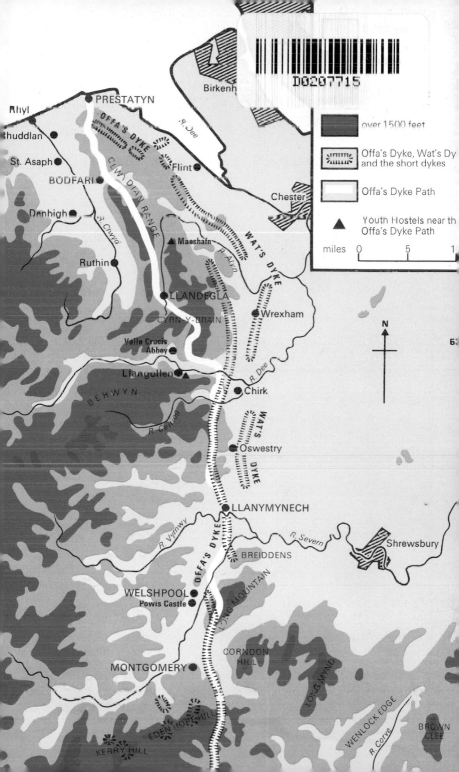

PRESTATYN

Rhyl

Rhuddlan

St. Asaph

BODFARI

Denbigh

Ruthin

Birkenh

R. Dee

Flint

Chester

D0207715

over 1500 feet

Offa's Dyke, Wat's Dy and the short dykes

Offa's Dyke Path

Youth Hostels near th Offa's Dyke Path

miles 0 5 1

OFFA'S DYKE

CLWYDIAN RANGE

R. Clwyd

Maeshafn

R. Alyn

WAT'S DYKE

LLANDEGLA

CYRN-Y-BRAIN

Wrexham

Valle Crucis Abbey

Llangollen

Chirk

R. Dee

BERWYN

R. Ceiriog

WAT'S DYKE

Oswestry

N

6:

LLANYMYNECH

R. Vyrnwy

R. Severn

Shrewsbury

BREIDDENS

OFFA'S DYKE

WELSHPOOL

Powis Castle

LONG MOUNTAIN

MONTGOMERY

CORNDON HILL

LONG MYND

EDEN HOPE HILL

WENLOCK EDGE

R. Corve

BROWN CLEE

KERRY HILL

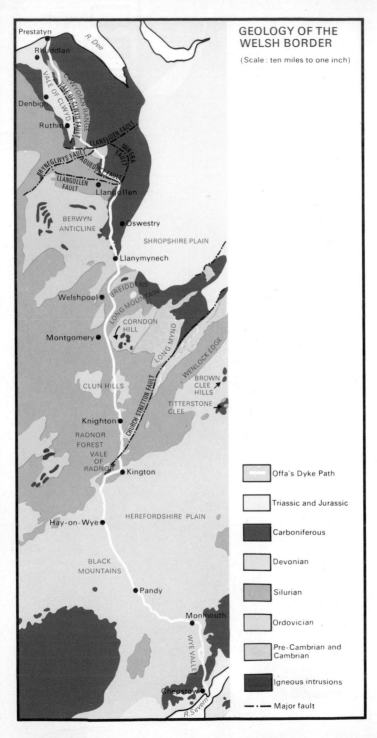

GEOLOGY OF THE WELSH BORDER

(Scale : ten miles to one inch)

Prestatyn

R. Dee

Rhuddlan

CLWYDIAN RANGE

VALE OF CLWYD

Denbigh

Ruthin

LLANELIDEN FAULT

MINERA FAULT

BRYNEGLWYS FAULT

AQUEDUCT FAULT

LLANGOLLEN FAULT

Llangollen

BERWYN ANTICLINE

Oswestry

SHROPSHIRE PLAIN

Llanymynech

BREIDDENS

Welshpool

LONG MOUNTAIN

CORNDON HILL

LONG MYND

Montgomery

WENLOCK EDGE

BROWN CLEE HILLS

CLUN HILLS

CHURCH STRETTON FAULT

TITTERSTONE CLEE

Knighton

RADNOR FOREST

VALE OF RADNOR

Kington

HEREFORDSHIRE PLAIN

Hay-on-Wye

BLACK MOUNTAINS

Pandy

Monmouth

WYE VALLEY

Chepstow

R. Severn

	Offa's Dyke Path
	Triassic and Jurassic
	Carboniferous
	Devonian
	Silurian
	Ordovician
	Pre-Cambrian and Cambrian
	Igneous intrusions
—·—·—	Major fault

ii

Offa's Dyke Path

John B. Jones

Long-Distance Footpath Guide No 4

London Her Majesty's Stationery Office
Published for the Countryside Commission

Front cover
Victorian tile from the floor of the choir in Hereford Cathedral,
depicting the beheading of St. Aethelbert by order of King Offa.
Reproduced by permission of the Dean and Chapter

Inside back cover
Pont-Cysyllte

Back cover
Mainstone Church

The maps in this guide are extracts from Ordnance Survey maps
1:25,000 or about 2½ inches to 1 mile and have been prepared from O.S.
Sheets SJ06, 07, 08, 15, 16, 20, 21, 22, 23, 24, 25; SO22, 23, 24, 25, 26,
27, 28, 29, 31, 32, 41, 50, 51; ST59

Drawings by John Western
Nature drawings by Harry Titcombe

© Crown copyright 1976
First published 1976

Government Bookshops

49 High Holborn, London WC1V 6HB
13a Castle Street, Edinburgh EH2 3AR
41 The Hayes, Cardiff CF1 1JW
Brazennose Street, Manchester M60 8AS
Southey House, Wine Street, Bristol BS1 2BQ
258 Broad Street, Birmingham B1 2HE
80 Chichester Street, Belfast BT1 4JY

Government publications are also available through booksellers

Prepared for the Countryside Commission by the
Central Office of Information

The waymark sign is used in
plaque or stencil form by the
Countryside Commission on
long-distance footpaths

**Long-Distance Footpath Guides published for the Countryside
Commission by HMSO:**
The Pennine Way, by Tom Stephenson: 120 pages, £1·50 net
The Cleveland Way, by Alan Falconer: 144 pages, £1·80 net
The Pembrokeshire Coast Path, by John H. Barrett: 124 pages,
£2·50 net

The following Guides are in preparation:
Cornwall Coast Path
Ridgeway Path

Printed in England for Her Majesty's Stationery Office by
Chorley & Pickersgill Ltd., Leeds.
ISBN 0 11 700350 6 Dd 288804 K80 2/76

Maps

Maps reference

Offa's Dyke Path ⟶ ① ━━━━━━

Waymarked Alternative Route ⎯ ⎯ ⎯ ⎯ ⎯

Map insets

These explain in greater detail complicated sections along the route and are based on information compiled by the author. Key to insets:

Fence	———————	Church	●
Wall	••••••••••••••	Buildings	■ ■
Broken Wall	....	Trees and Woodland	⣿
Hedge	ᴠᴠᴠᴠᴠᴠ	Offa's Dyke Signpost	●
Road	———————	Narrow Footpath or Intermittent Footpath	—·—·—·—
Broad Footpath or Track	— — — —	No Path Visible	··············

Class 1 Road	A40
„ 2 „	Fenced B4233 Unfenced
Roads Under Construction	= = = = = = = = = =
Other Roads	Good, metalled Poor, or unmetalled
Footpaths	*FP* Fenced *FP* Unfenced
Railways, Multiple Track	Station Road over Tunnel *FB* Cutting (Footbridge) Sidings
„ Single Track	Level Crossing Embankment Viaduct Road under
„ Narrow Gauge	
Aerial Ropeway	*Aerial Ropeway*
Boundaries, County or County Borough	— — — — —
„ „ „ „ „ with Parish	—·—·—·—·—
„ Parish	· · · · · · ·
Pipe Line (Oil, Water)	Pipe Line

Electricity Transmission Lines (Pylons shown at bends and spaced conventionally) – ⊗ – – – – ⊗ –

Post Offices (in Villages & Rural Areas only)	P	Town Hall	TH	Public House **PH**
Church or Chapel with Tower	⛪	Church or Chapel with Spire	⛪	Church or Chapel without either ✚
Triangulation Station	△	on Church with Tower	⬙	without Tower ⬙
Intersected Point on Chy	○	on Church with Spire	○	without Spire ✱ on Building ▬
Guide Post *GP.*	Mile Post *MP.*	Mile Stone *MS.*	Boundary Stone *BS* ○	Boundary Post *BP* ○
Youth Hostel Y	Telephone Call Box (Public) T	*(AA)* A	(RAC) R	Antiquity (site of) ✛

Public Buildings	▰	Glasshouses	▤
Quarry & Gravel Pit	⬭	Orchard	⬚
National Trust Area	Lydstep Point NT	Furze	⌢ ⌢ ⌢
Osier Bed	⁂	Rough Pasture Heath & Moor	·⸝· ·⸝·
Reeds	⁞	Marsh	⸺⸻
		Well	W ○
Park, Fenced	⬡	Spring	Spr ○

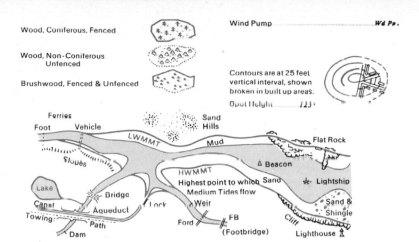

Wood, Coniferous, Fenced

Wood, Non-Coniferous
Untenced

Brushwood, Fenced & Unfenced

Wind Pump .... **Wd Pp.**

Contours are at 25 feet
vertical interval, shown
broken in built up areas.
Spot Height *125*

Ferries
Foot   Vehicle
LWMMT
Mud
Sand
Hills
Slopes
Flat Rock
△ Beacon
HWMMT
Highest point to which Sand
Medium Tides flow
⚓ Lightship
Lake
Bridge
Canal
Aqueduct
Lock
Weir
Sand &
Shingle
Towing
Path
Ford   FB
(Footbridge)
Cliff
Dam
Lighthouse

Place names

This glossary of place names is divided into those of Celtic origin
where the place-name components are given, with the addition of a
few complete names whose meaning is not too obvious; and into those
of essentially non-Celtic origin. Despite the apparent difficulty of
getting your tongue round words like Llwybr Clawdd Offa the
pronunciation of Welsh is in practice surprisingly straightforward.

The vowels are *a, e, i, o, u, w* and *y. A, e, i,* and *o* are long when they
carry a circumflex, or are followed by *b, ch, d, f, ff, g, s* or *th*; and short
when followed by two or more consonants or by *c, m, ng, p* or *t. U* takes
a short *ee* sound. *W* sounds like English *oo* as in *good. Y,* in syllables
other than the last, is like *u* in *pun;* in the last like *i* in *pin.* Hence
mynydd (mountain) = *mun-ith.* A number of the consonants differ in
pronunciation from English. *C, g,* and *s* are hard; *ch* as in Scottish
loch; dd (in *ddu*) as in *thee* (not as in *thick*); *f* is English *v; ff* is English *f;*
r is trilled; and for *ll* place your tongue behind your top teeth and hiss.
The stress is usually on the penultimate syllable. When looking for a
word in the glossary remember that certain consonants mutate:

b	mutates to	*f*	(*bach* to *fach*)	*c* mutates to *g*	(*craig* to *graig*)
d	,,	,, *dd* (*du*	,, *ddu*)	*ll* ,, ,, *l*	(*llwyd* ,, *lwyd*)
m	,,	,, *f*	(*mawr* ,, *fawr*)	*p* ,, ,, *b*	(*pandy* ,, *bandy*)
t	,,	,, *d*	(*tarren* ,, *darren*)		

Sometimes, too, the initial *g* is lost, e.g. *Fforddlas* (green way) =
ffordd + *glas; Y waun* (moor) = *y* + *gwaun.*

Glossary of Celtic Place Names

aber	river mouth, confluence, rivulet
afon	river
allt	steep hillside
bach	little, small
bedd (beddau)	grave(s)
Benlli	Dark Age tyrant, said to have held Moel Fenlli
betws	church
blaen	head, source
brân (brain)	crow(s)
bron	hillside
bwlch	pass
cae (caeau)	field(s)
caer	fortress
calch	limestone
carreg	stone, rock
castell	castle
cefn	ridge
Ceiriog	river belonging to Câr (doubtful)
celli	grove, copse
cilfach	corner, nook
clawdd (cloddiau)	hedge(s), bank(s), dyke(s)
Cnwclas	green mound
coch	red
coed	wood
collen	hazel wood
craig (creigiau)	rock(s), crags(s)
crib (cribau)	rugged crest(s)
croes	cross
cwm	coombe, valley
Cwmyoy	Cwm iau: vale of the yoke (because of its shape?)
cwrt	court
deri	oak
dinas	hill fortress, city
disgwylfa	viewpoint, look-out
dôl (dolau)	meadow(s)
du	black
esgob	bishop
Froncysyllte	junction on hillside
ffin	boundary
ffridd	lower part of hill or mountain, sheepwalk
ffynnon	well, spring
Gwaenysgor	camp on the moor
gwaun	moor, moorland, pasture
hafod	summer dwelling
helygen (helyg)	willow(s)
hen	old
hendre	winter dwelling
heol	road, street
isaf	lower, lowest
lladron	robbers
llan	enclosure, church
Llanarmon-yn-iâl	church of St Garmon iâl (Yale) = open space
Llandegla	church of St Tegla, said to have been converted by apostle Paul, martyred by Nero
llannerch	glade
Llanfair	church of St Mary
Llangollen	church of St Collen (see also collen)
Llanthony	"Llanddewi nant Hodni": church of Dewi at Hodni brook
Llantilio Crossenny	church of Teilio of Gresynnych? OR church of St Teilio + cross of honour
Llanvetherine	church of Gwytherin
Llangattock	church of Catwg
Llanfihangel	church of St Michael
Llanymynech	monastic church — where mynech = mynach OR village of minerals (?). Mynech as corruption of mwnau = minerals (?)
llech	slab, stone
llwybr	path
llwyd	grey, brown
llyn	lake
llys	herbs, berries; also mansion, court
maes	field
mawr	great
melin	mill
mochyn (moch)	pig(s)
moel	bare hill
mynach	monk
mynydd	mountain
nant	brook
newydd	new
ogof	cave
pandy	fulling mill
pen	head, top, end
plas	hall, mansion
pentre	village
pont	bridge
porth	gateway
pwll	pool
rhiw	slope, slant track
rhos	moorland
Rhuallt	steep hill
rhyd	ford
tan	until, below
tir	land, territory
tre, tref	homestead, hamlet, town

Trallwng		*uchaf*	upper, higher, highest
(*Welshpool*)	wet dell—as if greedily swallowing the surrounding waters	*y* (with consonant), *yr* (with vowel and "h")	
tomen	mound		
twyn	hillock, knoll	*'r* (after vowel)	the Definite Article
tŷ	house	*ystrad*	valley floor, strath, vale
tyddyn	smallholding		

Non-Celtic Place Names

Bodfari	possible site of Roman signal station of Variae
Brockweir	weir by the brook
Burfa	from *burf*, a fortified place
Buttington (Montgomeryshire)	Butta's farm? OR Bridge end, from a bridge over the Severn?
Chepstow	market place
Chirk	palatalised form of *Ceiriog*
Church Stoke	Place near to or belonging to a church
Clun	meaning is obscure
Clyro	meaning is obscure
Dolley Green	from Welsh *dolau*, meadows
Evenjobb	Emma's Valley? from *jobb* as a form of Mercian *hope*, valley; OR from *efes* (margin) and *hwpp* (slope)?
Forden	a shallow part of a river OR ford farm?
Gladestry	second element *treo(w)* = tree; first element probably a personal name
Grosmont	big hill (Norman French)
Hatterrall Hill	crown of the head hill; possibly a description of shape of hill given by Llanthony monks
Hay-on-Wye	from *haye* or *haie* = hedged enclosure

Kington	originally *Chingtune*; Howse suggests may have been so-called by Offa; royal farm?
Knighton	farm of the servants
Kymin	meaning is obscure
Lancaut	Church of St Cewydd
Leighton	herb garden
Lugg, River	light river
Lymore	fallow moor
Monmouth	mouth of River Monnow (Mynwy)
Montgomery	named after Roger de M's castle in Calvados
Oswestry	St Oswald's wooden cross
Prestatyn	priest's farm
Presteigne	priest's border?; OR border mead?
Radnor	red bank
Rushock Hill	Rushy brook hill?; but also *ock* = hope (valley)
Sedbury	Old Norse *setberg* = flat-topped hill
Severn	sluggish, thick river
Spoad	meaning is obscure
Tidenham	Dydda's river land
Tintern	from *din* (fortified hill) and perhaps *teyrn* (king)
Welshpool	the pool is probably the creek where the Lledin Brook joined the Severn, *Welsh* prefixed to distinguish from Dorset Pool
Wye	wandering river. Roman *Vaga*: the wanderer

Introduction

"I can't think why they brought the walk through here. There's a fine piece of Dyke two fields away, by that sycamore." It was one of the Border farmers talking. "But the chap from the local authority said the intention was to provide a pleasant walk, and not to follow the Dyke all the way."

While Offa's Dyke is the theme for the path, there are many miles where the route detours from its course to give a scenically more attractive walk. Many may come to the Offa's Dyke Path after the Pennine Way, and comparisons will inevitably be made. But the fact is the Dyke Path does not stand comparison: it is just different. Only two sections, the Black Mountains and the Clwydians, are truly comparable in offering really open walking country. For the rest the appeal lies in landscapes of a more varied and intricate character, from the high and open hill country of the Clun district, through the rolling cultivated country of foothills, and the thickly wooded Wye Valley, to the pastoral landscape of the Monmouthshire lowlands and the level flood plain of the Severn.

Offa's Dyke Path (Llwybr Clawdd Offa), Britain's fourth long-distance footpath to be officially opened, runs the entire length of the Border, from the Severn Estuary near Chepstow in the south, to the sea at Prestatyn in the north, an official distance of 168 miles. Throughout its length history is brought to life, not just by Offa's frontier earthwork, but by ancient hill forts, prehistoric trackways, old drove roads; by medieval castles set up to guard the English plain against descents by Welsh hillmen, and by the small market towns and villages which the path links.

As a footpath rich in scenic variety, and historic and literary associations, and as a route readily accessible by car and to a lesser extent public transport, it will have attractions for not just the seasoned walker, completing the coast-to-coast walk in two or three weeks, but also the amateur historian and archaeologist; the motorist seeking a change from driving; those who welcome the possibility of walking the Dyke in short sections over a period of time; and those who come to it out of mere curiosity or discover it by accident.

The path was approved by the Minister of Housing and Local Government in 1955 but little progress was made for some years in opening up the many miles of new rights of way needed, partly because the local authorities were preoccupied at that time with other, more pressing, problems. But, in 1966, the then National Parks Commission decided to give greater priority to the proposal, and began to give the local councils more active encouragement and help on the work.

At national level, the Commission at that time had no powers to create new footpaths. The responsibility for approving proposals lay with the Minister of Housing and Local Government. At local government level, the job of creating new rights of way could be undertaken by either the county or the district councils, while the responsibility for making the paths operational through the provision of stiles and general clearance lay with the highway authorities, normally the county councils.

Then, in 1969, a year after the National Parks Commission became the Countryside Commission, came a proposal to open the path officially during 1971. The Offa's Dyke Association, set up to promote interest in, and conservation of, the Border area along the path, and to work for the eventual completion of the route, were understandably sceptical. However, the local authorities concerned went ahead with their work of consulting landowners and of clearing and signposting the path. With a few exceptions the route had been completed and waymarked by the target date. On 10 July 1971, Lord Hunt formally opened the path at an open-air ceremony in Knighton, the opening being preceded by an inaugural walk along part of the path north of the town over Panpunton Hill. This event was combined with another ceremony for the dedication of an Offa's Dyke Park to the town of Knighton by Lady Green-Price.

Naval Temple, the Kymin

Geology

Throughout the Welsh Border the contrast between upland and lowland caused by the different underlying rocks marks not just a physical boundary but one that has played a key role in the course of historical events. As you can read in the next chapter it is a boundary across which, over the centuries, tides of movement of Man the conqueror and Man the conquered have swept back and forth. Except in Salop, where an extensive hill mass pushes well out into England, a gentle arc drawn from Prestatyn in the north to Newport in the south would roughly separate upland from lowland.

There could be little better introduction to the rocks along the Dyke Path than Sedbury Cliff. Here the successive strata of the Keuper series represent the youngest rocks along the whole walk, laid down when the climate was hot and arid and the British land mass only 300 miles or so from the Equator. Over 50 feet of Red Marl give way to 10 feet of Tea Green Marls, in turn to nearly 20 feet of Rhaetic Beds whose black shale band, the Bone Bed, partly obscured by the trees of the cliff, is a richly fossiliferous stratum which has revealed the remains of Ichthyosaurus and Pleisiosaurus in the cliffs of Aust across the Severn. Finally come nearly 40 feet of Lower Lias.

In the short mile across the Beachley Peninsula the rock has changed to Carboniferous Limestone which characterises the first miles of the Wye Valley. To the east of the Valley this limestone almost completely surrounds the Coal Measures of the Forest of Dean plateau. From here it extends south-west in the Tidenham Chase syncline to Chepstow, and westward towards Newport. Through it the Wye has downcut an impressive course, forming high cliffs.

Near Tintern you go back further in geological history as limestone gives way to Old Red Sandstone. Apart from a small outlier of limestone on Highbury Plain, Old Red Sandstone forms the underlying rock for the next 50 miles or so, although different series give rise to markedly different terrain. Through Redbrook the Wye has cut a narrow steep-sided valley; around Monmouth the Valley opens out across alluvial flats and river terrace gravels; while between Monmouth and Abergavenny the Ditton and Downton series of the Old Red Sandstone, overlain in many places by glacial lake clay, form an undulating tract of land, rising in places to more prominent hills, but dipping gradually northwards to the broad plain of Hereford.

The Brecon series, by contrast, forms the impressive high ridges of the Black Mountains. This series contains two of the most resistant of the Devonian formations: the Brownstones and the Plateau Beds. The Brownstones, layer upon layer of them, red marls, brown sandstones

3

and conglomerates, form the dominant rock, the harder beds standing out as steps and shelves — the darrens. The Plateau Beds form the cappings of conglomerate and sandstone that give the well-known flat tops. In the great scarp at the north end of the Mountains, overlooking the Wye Valley, the Brownstones are over 1,000 feet thick.

The Offa's Dyke Path descends from the mountains and crosses the alluvial flats of the middle Wye Valley to the Radnorshire Hills. At Newchurch, in the valley of the Arrow, a transition begins to the rocks of the Silurian Period which dominate until Llanymynech is reached. In Silurian times a basin of deepish water and subsidence north-west of a line from Radnor to the south end of Ape Dale gave way to a broad shelf to the south-east where reefs built up. The present-day scenery in the basin area is predominantly of bold rounded hills across which the long-distance path runs, while the limestones of the shelf area form conspicuous scarp features, such as Wenlock Edge.

One of the geologically most interesting areas along the path is the Vale of Radnor, In this area, associated with the continuation southwards of the Church Stretton Fault, Silurian strata rest unconformably on Longmyndian rocks of Pre-Cambrian age. A triangle of Wenlockian strata forms the level fertile Vale. On the south-east side, within the continuation of the Church Stretton Fault, lie some of the oldest hills along the whole Border. Old Radnor Hill is composed of Pre-Cambrian grits with bands of conglomerate which give rise to the crags on its summit. Hanter Hill, Worsell Wood and Stanner Rocks are igneous (dolerite and gabbro), again of Pre-Cambrian origin. The Ludlovian siltstones of the high upland of the Radnor Forest to the west of the Vale form a distinctive profile seen for many miles around.

Through the catchment areas of the Lugg, Teme and Clun the path pursues its way across a dissected hill country where Silurian rocks (Ludlovian) continue to dominate, with large outliers of Downtonian rocks of the Old Red Sandstone forming the more elevated tracts of land. From Edenhope Hill in the Clun district a wide panorama takes in the complete series of vales and hills that extends across south Salop. The sprawling synclinal mass of the Long Mountain to the north is due to the relatively soft Upper Silurians. The great dolerite laccolith of Corndon Hill is unmistakable. Residual Arenig Quartzite in the Stiperstones Ridge forms conspicuous summit crags. The extensive plateau of the Long Mynd is next in the scene, a vast thickness of Pre-Cambrian grits, flags and conglomerates. Brown Clee and Titterstone Clee, 20 miles away, are remains of Coal Measures protected by cappings of dolerite.

The dull flats of the Severn are relieved by the isolated Breidden Hills, resistant igneous rocks folded into a laccolith. The Breidden itself is predominantly of dolerite, Moel-y-golfa is capped by andesite, and Middletown Hill is of a volcanic conglomerate. Behind Llanymynech the Carboniferous Limestone comes to an abrupt end through faulting. From here the Carboniferous rocks extend northward along the Border through Clwyd, giving rise, along their gently dipping western margins, to scarp and dip features. The most notable is the west-facing limestone scarp from Llanymynech, via Moelydd, to the Vale of Llangollen, continuing as the towering

Eglwyseg Crags. Eastwards the younger Carboniferous rocks show less marked scarp features as they descend to the Cheshire and Shropshire Plains to become buried beneath the Keuper Marls and Bunter Sandstones.

The Carboniferous series of Clwyd provide the economically most productive measures along the Border. In the vicinity of Llanymynech and Nant Mawr the limestone is extensively quarried. Mining in the area goes back to Roman times when zinc, lead, copper, silver and especially lime were sought. The Coal Measures underlying the built-up industrial belt between Oswestry and the Dee Estuary have been worked for ironstone, fireclay and ganister, as well as coal.

The hills to the west of the Carboniferous Limestone scarp are Ordovician in origin. They form the foothills of the Berwyn mass, an anticlinal dome composed principally of sandstones, mudstones and shales, and rising to 2,713 feet in Moel Sych. In the Vale of Llangollen area the geology is complicated by a series of faults associated with the Hercynian earth movements that followed the Carboniferous period.

These movements were responsible for the great crags of Trevor and Eglwyseg on the north side of the Vale. The limestone, resistant to weathering, stands out as vertical rock face. Weathering of the scarp face during the Ice Ages and perhaps earlier resulted in the extensive clayey scree and boulder slopes at the foot of the crags. On the plateau top of the Eglwyseg Mountain limestones give way to a capping of gritstone, the Cefn Sandstone.

The prominent knoll of Dinas Brân which you pass near Trevor Rocks is largely of Silurian mudstone. The rolling moors of Cyrn-y-brain, shales with thin sandy bands of Ordovician origin, are crossed on your way northwards. In the Alyn Gap beyond, the major Bryneglwys Fault running south-westward has allowed river and ice erosion to remove the weakened beds associated with it. Here the Morwynion and Alyn Rivers flow in opposite directions with little divide.

The Silurian hills of the Clwydian Range, uplifted by the same movements that displaced the limestone of the Eglwyseg Rocks, form a narrow range bounded on the east by the Carboniferous series of the Flintshire Coalfield, and on the west by the Vale of Clwyd, where the Vale of Clwyd Fault is the reason for the steep scarp on this side. Against this fault occur small outcrops of Carboniferous Limestone. During the Mesozoic era the whole of the Flintshire and Denbighshire Coalfields were beneath the waters of an extensive lake. The Vale, in existence at this time, was also filled with water. Here Triassic New Red Sandstone rests in places on Upper, and in places on Lower, Carboniferous rocks. It is thought that in the lower reaches of the Vale the Coal Measures may exist at sufficiently shallow depth for coal to be workable.

For the last miles of the path, beyond Rhuallt, the Silurians which have so far flanked the Vale give way to Carboniferous Limestone.

Harry Titcombe

Border history

The Welsh Borderland is a contact area. Here Welsh and English people and cultures meet and mingle, and the result is not a weaker but a more robust product.

Dorothy Sylvester

The Celtic Invasion

I have chosen to begin this brief account of Border history with the coming of the Celtic peoples into Britain from about 1000 B.C., for it is only with their coming that we begin to see the first signs of a Border developing. Following in the wake of these earlier Celtic settlers came a wave of more sophisticated Celts, skilled in ironcraft. From Brittany they spread, during the third century B.C. to the first century A.D., into Ireland and west and north Britain. Although these people had, it seems, a common language and religion, they formed no compact state, existing as separate tribes, each under its own leader, often at war with one another. Their most permanent traces along the Border are found today in the many hill forts they established.

The multiple ramparts of these forts you can see enclosing the summits of prominent hills and knolls would originally have been faced with timber or stone, surmounted by a timber palisade, and guarded by watch-towers. Inside the ramparts would be huts of turf, timber-roofed, usually circular, and as much as 60 feet across. The forts, built probably as strongholds, retreats for the inhabitants in time of danger, or as more permanent homes during prolonged warfare, such as the Roman invasions, bear witness to the spartan way of life that must have prevailed.

Archaeological finds in the forts show these people were skilled not just in iron, but in bronze, gold and enamel. They used chariots in battle and were a formidable fighting people, as the Romans were to discover, "war-mad and . . . quick for battle, otherwise simple and uncouth", as one contemporary Roman writer described them.

The Roman Invasion

The Romans' advance, in the early stages of their invasion, was rapid, so that by A.D. 47 they had reached westward to the Severn. Ahead lay the hill country, defended by strong British tribes: the warlike Silures of the south under their Belgic leader Caradog (Caractacus) who had fled westward to rouse the Britons of the west; the Ordovices of the central Border; and the Deceangli of the north. Caradog was defeated in A.D. 51, and many places along the Border claim to be the site of his last battle. Strong resistance continued, however, through the Border, and it was ten years before the Romans could bend their attack to the Ordovices and Deceangli, following the establishment in A.D. 60 of the fortress and legionary headquarters of Deva (Chester). Only a year later the army had advanced to Anglesey, overrunning the hill forts. In the south the campaign of A.D. 74 was the decisive one when Julius Frontinius fought a hard battle against the Silures, though it was four years before the Romans could move west under Agricola.

The Border formed very much a frontier zone in Roman expansion. Except in the south, in the Wye Valley area, and east of the hill margin, developments were essentially military in character, with no great effect on native life, which went on much as before. Roads linking the several forts that had been set up in this zone ran along the north and south coast routes, based on Deva and Isca (Caerleon), and east–west up the main valleys into the hills, the easiest routes into what was to become Wales. A north–south road linked these roads along the Border. During the first century of Roman rule a number of the Celtic hill forts were strengthened, for although the Celts had made use of the sharp upland-lowland edge, its strategic possibilities were first realised by the Romans as a base for launching their campaigns against the uplands. The Roman roads and fortifications defined for the first time in history a Welsh Border.

The Dark Ages

With the withdrawal of the Romans in A.D. 410, Celtic culture saw a renaissance in craftsmanship and bardic poetry, accompanied by a growth in political power and the rise and spread of Christianity in the Celtic Church. Gradually various Welsh kingdoms began to emerge under separate rulers. Along the Border the kingdom of Gwynedd covered the land north of the Dee and west of the Vale of Clwyd. The Vale itself formed a debatable territory between Gwynedd and the great central kingdom of Powys, the Paradise of Wales as the bard Llywarch Hen called it. On the southern Border Brycheiniog covered roughly the former county of Brecon, and Gwent, Monmouthshire.

In Powys was a great centre of poetry and here we find reference to Taliesin singing at the court.

"I sang in the meadows of the Severn
Before an illustrious lord,
Before Brochfael of Powys. . . ."

It seems to have been usual for an official bard to be attached to each court, some courts and princes acquiring reputations as patrons of the bards.

In 577 Ceawlin, king of Wessex, had driven a wedge between the Britons dwelling between the Bristol Channel and the Irish Sea and those in Devon and Cornwall. A second wedge, driven by Aethelfrith, king of all Northumbria, early in the seventh century, and separating the Britons in Cumbria from their compatriots further south, effectively isolated and created Wales. Between 650–670 Anglo-Saxon advance westward towards Wales had reached the middle and north Border, while the Wye marked the limit of advance in the south. During the seventh century Northumbria was the most powerful of the Anglo-Saxon heptarchy. The ascendancy of the midland kingdom of Mercia began during the reign of the warlike and pagan Penda (623–654). Minor kings after him rose and fell in a period of fighting. By 731, Bede tells us, all England south of the Humber was subject to Aethelbald (716–756). For 30 years he maintained his ascendancy until he was murdered by his own bodyguard. From the ensuing civil war in Mercia there emerged the key figure in Mercian supremacy, and the key figure to the long-distance path.

Offa reigned from 757–796, achieving unprecedented power in southern England. Whereas Aethelbald had called himself King of the southern English, Offa was the first ruler to be styled King of the English. Throughout the first half of the eighth century a protracted struggle had gone on along the Border as the frontier was gradually driven back from the line of furthest advance marked by various short dykes, to the more settled frontier marked by the great running earthwork of Offa's Dyke, constructed probably after the last Welsh attack in 784. Offa and the Dyke form the subjects of the next chapter.

The ninth to eleventh centuries saw various attempts to create a wider unity in Wales as from time to time powerful leaders emerged: Rhodri Mawr, for instance (844–878); and Hywel Dda, his grandson, who brought together the customs of the various areas he had consolidated under the Law of Hywel Dda. The early decades of the eleventh century were troubled times when usurpers like Llywelyn ap Seisyll (1018–1023) seized power. With his son Gruffydd ap Llywelyn the whole of Wales came under single rule for the first time.

With Gruffydd's death in 1063 Wales was disunited once more, but Harold, on succeeding Edward the Confessor on the English throne, was forced to turn his back on Wales and put all his efforts to the defence of his own claim to the throne against William of Normandy.

The Norman Conquest

Norman conquest of strife-torn Wales, though piecemeal, served only to intensify Welsh disunity, as the Norman lords, advancing by the easier valley routes, or on the lines of the old Roman roads, conducted private campaigns from their newly acquired English estates. A little further east William established three great strategic centres, from which the Normans could advance into the Border. From Hereford, set up in 1066 and based on the cathedral settlement, important even in Offa's time, went William Fitzosbern, establishing Border castles at Wigmore, Clifford and Ewyas Harold, at Chepstow and later Caerleon. From Shrewsbury, set up in 1071, but dating from the time of Aethelfleda, Roger de Montgomery, over the lords of Caus, Sai and Oswestry, proved a constant threat in the middle Border to Powys. From William's third strategic centre at Chester (1071), on the site of Roman Deva, Hugh d'Avranches opened a route into North Wales, enabling Robert of Rhuddlan to press forward to gain lands of his own and set up his castle at Rhuddlan.

By the end of the eleventh century the Welsh Border had undergone unprecedented political change. The Normans of the March who had gained their lands by private conquest ruled virtually autonomously. In these lands the king had little right to interfere. Many of the large number of castles that now existed up and down the March were therefore fortified centres of government, each lordship having one main castle and usually other castles the centres of sub-lordships.

At first the castles were of the simple motte and bailey type; but, with increased Welsh attack, were strengthened. On each lordship the lord developed certain lands as a manor on the feudal system, the tenants who farmed the lands paying in money or kind for their homestead and share of the plots. The Norman system of castle, manor and borough was dominant in the lowland areas where Norman advance had been most effective. Weekly markets and yearly or twice-yearly fairs were now a feature of life where the country folk could trade. The areas administered in this way constituted the Englishries. In contrast, in the Welshries, the more hilly areas, the Welsh by and large retained their own way of life based on the Law of Hywel Dda, but paid tribute to the Norman lord.

12th to 16th Centuries

The changes of power in the Border at this time are complex and I can do no more here than outline the main trends. Professor William Rees's *An Historical Atlas of Wales* is very readable for anyone wishing to extend his knowledge of Border history in general.

The twelfth century saw a continuing and accelerated opening up of the land along the Border, many of the great woodland areas being cleared to make way for agriculture, and to provide timber for housing, fuel and ships. These decades saw also the growth of townships around the Norman castles. Today the Border contains a fascinating variety of towns in various stages of development. A number of the early motte and bailey castles are now no more than a steep mound, like Nantcribbau near Montgomery. Around other castles, like White Castle, the townships never developed, while around such as Grosmont the beginnings of a town are clear. Monmouth is a township that grew into a small market town, while Oswestry grew into an important sub-regional centre.

From the twelfth century to the time of the Wars of the Roses history is characterised by wave after wave of Welsh uprisings as strong leaders emerged, intent on uniting Wales. There was Llywelyn ap Iorwerth (The Great), supported by the English barons against King John, and against the Welsh rulers who feared Llywelyn's advance; and his grandson, Llywelyn ap Gruffydd who gained control of Powys.

Gradually, too, in this period we see a decline in the power of the Marcher lordships. The king, for the first time, and no doubt concerned at Marcher autonomy as much as by any wish to hold sway over the Welsh, begins to acquire lands of his own in Wales.

The two wars of independence (1276 and 1282) resulting from Llywelyn's refusal to pay homage to Edward I, culminated in the confiscation of all Llywelyn's lands. The royal hold on Wales, now extending over the north and west of the country, was accompanied by a second great phase of castle building. Arrangements for the government of the new Crown lands were laid down in the Treaty of Rhuddlan. Although there was no drastic change in the customs of the people, and the tribal and clan groupings still existed, these were slowly to break down over the following centuries. In 1301 Edward granted all the Welsh Crown lands to his eldest son, now called the Prince of Wales.

Through the years up to 1400 strong undercurrents of discontent needed only the emergence of a strong leader to unite Wales in rebellion. Much has been written for and against Owain Glyndŵr who appeared as leader of the Welsh in 1400. But he was without doubt a man of insight and vision, for had the rebellion succeeded Wales could at that time have had its own Church and university. The revolt, originating from a quarrel between Glyndŵr and Lord Grey of Ruthin over the boundary of their territories, soon developed into widespread national revolt. Glyndŵr was strongly backed by discontented elements in England, hostile to Henry IV's usurpation of the throne from Richard II.

The defeat of the Welsh at the Battles of Usk and Grosmont in 1405, and the speedy return home of the French forces sent by Charles VI to support Glyndŵr, were serious blows to the Welsh cause. By 1409 the revolt had been crushed, leaving behind widespread destruction and a country broken by the demands of the state for lost revenues.

By the time of the Wars of the Roses, with Crown territories spread throughout Wales and the Marcher lordships with less power, the strategic importance of the Border had greatly diminished.

The Union of England and Wales

Not until the Wars of the Roses had meant that many of the lordships had passed to the Crown, could the king establish a council of the Marches of Wales (1471), which continued to function, if intermittently, until the time of Henry VIII and the Acts of Union in 1536 and 1542, binding England and Wales into a single state.

Offa and the Dyke

Within two myles, there is a famous thing,
Cal'de Offa's dyke, that reacheth farre in length.

Thomas Churchyard: Worthiness of Wales (1587)

History reveals all too little of the Mercian king, Offa, who reigned from 757–796 over the powerful midland kingdom of the Anglo-Saxon heptarchy. From the civil war in Mercia that followed the murder of Aethelbald, he emerged as king, achieving unprecedented power in southern England as his kingdom was gradually expanded, not always, it seems, by fair means.

In 793 Aethelbert, king of East Anglia, on a visit to Offa seeking the hand of his daughter Aelfrida, was murdered, either by Offa or by his queen. There are different accounts of what happened, but it is most likely that with Aethelbert out of the way Mercia could take over East Anglia, which it did. Offa was able to deal on almost equal terms with Charlemagne who at one time closed his ports to English trade for some three years.

As I said in the last chapter, not until 784 were relatively peaceful times along the Border achieved. It is during the latter years, then, of Offa's reign that the Dyke that bears his name almost certainly will have been constructed.

Around this time we can picture the English as settled farmers, with greater craftsmanship and better equipment than their fifth- and sixth-century predecessors, if with less military skill. The Welsh in the hill zone to the west, living in kinship groups (gwelau), were dependent mainly upon the cattle they summer-pastured on the hills and over-wintered on the lowlands.

The line of the Dyke extends from Sedbury Cliffs on the Severn, through the Wye Valley and the county of Hereford, across the Clun district of Salop, and northwards via Chirk and Ruabon to the sea at Prestatyn, a distance of 149 miles. The running earthwork of the Dyke itself is traceable for 81 miles. It consists of an earth bank, ditched, usually on the west side, sometimes on both, and averaging in height some six feet above ground level, and in breadth almost 60 feet. While contemporary material throws little light on the making of the Dyke, Sir Cyril Fox's masterly treatise, *Offa's Dyke: A Field Survey of the Western Frontier Works of Mercia in the Seventh and Eighth Centuries*

Chepstow Castle from Rennie's iron bridge

A.D., the result of a detailed survey of the Dyke, has led to a much deeper understanding of the Border as it existed in Offa's day.

Its Purposes

The principal purposes of the Dyke were as a frontier between Mercia and the Welsh kingdoms, and to control trade by directing movement across the Border to defined routeways through the earthwork. It may have had an additional defensive purpose, but this would be incidental. The Dyke may too have served as an obstacle to cattle raiders, though it would scarcely have prevented cattle from straying across. Only unchallengeable power would allow such a great undertaking, and only in a climate of relative peace between Wales and Mercia could a work of such a scale be achieved. In other words, it must have been an agreed frontier.

Precedents

The sheer mastery of often difficult terrain through which the Dyke runs suggests the skill of its builders can only have been acquired through generations of experience. Two precedents on the ground are to be found, firstly in the various short dykes that lie to both east and west of the Dyke, and secondly in Wat's Dyke running from Holywell to Maesbury, south of Oswestry. A third precedent lies in heroic poetry.

The short dykes found throughout the middle Border controlled the most vulnerable zone where the hills of Salop most nearly approach the Mercian capital of Tamworth. In construction these dykes are similar to Offa's Dyke. The cross-valley dykes, Fox argues, formed protective screens at the head of agricultural land, while the 13

THE KINGS OF MERCIA

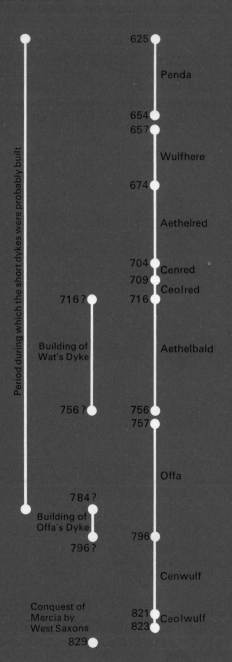

Period during which the short dykes were probably built

625 — Penda
654
657 — Wulfhere
674 — Aethelred
704 — Cenred
709 — Ceolred
716

716 ? — Building of Wat's Dyke — 756 ?

Aethelbald

756
757 — Offa

784 ? — Building of Offa's Dyke — 796 ?

796 — Cenwulf

821 — Ceolwulf
823

Conquest of Mercia by West Saxons
829

cross-ridge dykes controlled traffic along the ridge. The short dykes probably date from the time of Penda and represent the military activities of Mercia in the pre-Offan period. They are defensive, unlike Offa's Dyke which represents a consolidation of the Mercian kingdom when the lowlanders realised the limits of their ability to advance.

Historic evidence points to Wat's Dyke as an attempt to mark a boundary and defence covering the heart of Mercia. Most likely the work of Aethelbald, it probably marks the first boundary Mercia was able to establish.

Wat was a hero of Old English legend associated with an earlier Offa, a king in Sleswig and ancestor to the Mercian Offa. Wat's Dyke may well have been named by Offa after the hero associated with his own namesake, for there is more than just a possibility that Offa II modelled his own life on the deeds of Offa I, recorded in the poem *Widsith* as a marker of boundaries.

Planning and Control of the Dyke

Evidence shows that the Dyke was built under the direction of men trained in military tradition. Offa, perhaps with a group of chiefs, master-minded the work, planning its course and dimensions. Then, it appears, each landowner along the Border would have been responsible for a particular length of Dyke according to the extent of his lands or the labour resources available to him. The differing experience and expertise, the will to work and the size of the work force would account to a large extent for variations in construction and scale of the earthwork. In some areas, too, presumably there would be harassment from the Welsh.

Offa's Dyke, as a boundary, was unlikely ever to have been continuously manned, but it was probably patrolled on horseback. Further evidence that it was an agreed frontier is contained in the apparent existence of a set of laws governing the movements of Welsh and English across the Border. An early tenth-century document refers to an agreement between the English and the Welsh relating to Archenfield, a Welsh district between the Wye and Monnow, and English territory north of the Wye, forming together a people known as the Dunsaete. The ordinance suggests the existence of a relationship between these peoples that may well have dated from the time of Offa, and have derived from Offa's own laws for the conduct of the Welsh and English along the Border.

Offa's laws, long thought lost, would then have provided for the setting-up of a "board" of English and Welsh to explain the laws to their people. Included in the laws: a code for recovering stock rustled across the Border; another for the safe conduct of either Welshman or Mercian on the "wrong" side of the Border by a specially appointed guide. The story that any man found illegally on the wrong side of the Dyke would lose his right hand is apocryphal.

The Alignment

The skill of the designer and eye for country shown by the purposeful alignment of the Dyke are remarkable. With few exceptions, even in the dissected terrain of the middle Border, the Dyke, set out in a series of broadly straight lengths, seeks out west-facing slopes giving visual control over Wales.

In a fascinating piece of archaeological detective work, Fox's study of the alignment of the Dyke enabled him to map the character of the Border landscape in Offa's day. Straight alignments of the Dyke, occurring in flat or undulating country, indicate a landscape of pastoral or arable farming; and in upland, open moorland. Small irregularities in a broadly straight alignment tend to indicate that the course of the Dyke lay through woodland. The Mercian farmers' predilection for sunny, south-facing slopes for crops, and dislike of shaded north-facing hillsides which remained wooded is well demonstrated by the respective straight and sinuous alignments. Very irregular alignments, with the Dyke following the contours of the land, occur where the terrain is especially bold, or where visibility between two points was very limited.

In the crossing of major valleys skilful use is made of the east sides of lateral valleys such that the Dyke descends from ridge to valley floor while still maintaining visual control to the west.

Profile of the Dyke

In section the Dyke varies considerably throughout its length. It is at its most formidable on hill tops where ridgeways passed through, and on valley floors where cultivated clearings demanded protection in the tradition of the short dykes. Elsewhere, away from these key points, the Dyke is usually much smaller in scale, serving only to link the massive sections in the delineation of a boundary.

Concessions to the Welsh

In many places it appears the Dyke was the result of compromise. For example, while north of Buttington the Severn formed the boundary, to the south, where it could equally well have formed the frontier line, the boundary is marked by a length of Dyke on the slopes of the Long Mountain to the east. This suggests the concession of the Severn pastures to Powys, for it is told in *The Mabinogion* that "the man would not prosper with a war-band in Powys who would not prosper in that cultivated land".

In the Wye Valley the river seems to have been used by Welsh timber traders who would need to land boats on either bank. It would have been politically unwise to make the river the boundary as farther north in Herefordshire. The Dyke is therefore high up on the eastern slope, controlling the Wye as far upstream as the point reached by exceptionally high tides at Redbrook.

Place Names

This concession to the Welsh along the Wye is borne out by the late survival of Welsh-speaking Archenfield and the abundance of Celtic place-name elements west of the Wye. Around Welshpool names like Buttington, Forden and Leighton show Mercian expansion to the Border between 650 and 750 and strengthen the case for the concession of the Severn meadows to Powys with the building of the Dyke. In the Vale of Radnor area, names like Evenjobb, Harpton and Cascob again indicate a retreat. Elsewhere on the whole the land bordering the Dyke is a transition zone between English and Welsh elements.

Tintern Abbey

'Missing' Portions

For much of the length of the frontier no trace of the Dyke has been found. From the point where the Dyke reaches the Wye west of Sedbury Cliffs, to the Wye west of the Tutshill look-out tower, the sheer river cliffs will have formed sufficient natural boundary in themselves. Between Highbury and Bridge Sollers in Herefordshire the Wye again forms the boundary. For the next 13 miles to Rushock Hill ancient and dense oakwoods on the underlying Old Red Sandstone seem to have made the building of a Dyke unnecessary, if not impossible. In this area the Dyke is present only on what would have been cleared land. For five miles north of Buttington on the Severn the river again forms the boundary.

Why the Dyke was never completed in the last miles to the sea in the north is a matter of conjecture. Certainly the intention was that it *should* reach the sea. Perhaps Welsh harassment made work impossible, or the workmen responsible for this section had no inclination to work. We know that towards the end of Offa's reign the Welsh seem to have made an attempt to capture the land between the Dyke and the Dee. A Welsh tradition, handed down in legend and in the plaintive lament *Morfa Rhuddlan*, tells of a fierce battle fought in 795, ending in Welsh defeat.

Offa died a year later at Rhuddlan, and it may be that with him went the driving force behind the Dyke.

The Dyke Today

Offa was succeeded by his son, Cenwulf, who reigned until 816. His defeat at the Battle of Basingwerk marked the beginning of the decline of Mercian supremacy on the Border. Wessex was now emerging as the most powerful Saxon kingdom, and Mercia was forced to turn its attention to the south. With the Dyke established, however, a degree of stability was brought to the Border for a time.

In the succeeding centuries, developments along the Border have changed the character as well as the function of the earthwork. It has been used as a means of communication, by footpath and track, country lane and major road. Few of the present-day gaps in the Dyke, filled by modern roads or farm tracks, are original, though occasionally roads and tracks do lie on original routeways that have been widened. On valley floors flooding and river action have often removed the Dyke altogether. North of Llanymynech it has been destroyed by quarrying and, on the fringe of Chepstow, mutilated by housing development.

A number of farmsteads have become associated with the Dyke (Middle Knuck in the Clun district, and Pen Offa near Chirk are but two), also villages (Llanymynech is half in England, half in Wales), and even towns (Knighton is called in Welsh Tref-y-clawdd: the town by the Dyke).

Today some of the best preserved sections are in limestone country where the ditch remains well defined, the bank steep and narrow. In areas of sandy soil the Dyke has tended to spread, and in clayey soil erosion has invariably levelled the Dyke to a low, broad mound running through the landscape. In places natural erosion has been helped along by ploughing.

For some of its course the Dyke marks present local government boundaries, or more locally the boundaries to farms. But while, for the most part, the political boundary between England and Wales no longer follows it, the Dyke remains the symbolic frontier, "because there is a natural limit to the territory of a highland people and the Dyke is the only visible and historic structure which corresponds reasonably well to that fundamental reality".

Some notes on wild life

Just as the underlying geology influenced the shaping of Man's history on the Border, so it has determined the many different wild life communities to be found along the Dyke Path. I could not hope here to give a detailed description of each community along the Border, but rather to note some of the more dominant species which are there for all to see, and a few of the less common species which you may not see, but which none the less are integral parts of their own communities.

One of the richest areas on the Border is the Wye Valley, famous for the beech and oak that clothe its slopes, and for the giant yews on Highbury Plain. Well known too for the bluebells in spring that carpet the floors of the woods for mile upon mile, the Wye Valley is a splendid beginning to the long-distance path. Wild garlic has colonised large areas of these mature woods, making the air pungent with its distinctive odour (not to everyone's liking). In woodland not long cleared, broom forms an attractive shrub layer. Here and there groups of the Early Purple Orchid *(Orchis mascula)* are to be found beside the path (where they should be left!), and even on the Dyke itself.

Of the creatures that inhabit these woods you will be lucky indeed to catch sight of a badger, but may, if on the look-out, spot one or more badger runs. Among the woodland insects are the magnificent Silver-Washed Fritillary and the White Admiral. The Wye itself is noted among rivers for its salmon and trout (a speciality of many restaurants in the area). In summer, as you follow its banks to Bigsweir you will find the air heady with the smell of Indian Balsam *(Impatiens glandulifera)*.

In its own distinctive way the middle Border is almost as rich in wild life. Here again it is the bluebells that carpet the Dyke that will be one of the most memorable features of a spring walk. In summer it is the invasive bracken *(Pteridium aquilinum)* that you are more likely to remember, if only for the obstruction it causes. On the high hills of Radnorshire and the Clun district the mewing cry of the buzzard is a familiar sound as the bird circles overhead. The wheeling lapwing is easily recognised by its flapping flight. On Rhosgoch Common, above Newchurch, at the head of the Arrow, is a well-known breeding ground of the black-headed gull.

In some areas of the Border rabbits have made a come-back. Offa can scarcely have foreseen that his Dyke would prove ideal for these creatures to colonise. As a result, of course, parts of the earthwork have partly collapsed. A word of caution then to be wary of the ankle-twisting propensities of these sections of Dyke!

In the Clun district increased afforestation has meant the loss of a number of bird species and a curtailment of the old sheep runs. None 19 the less these rolling uplands are still grazed by the Kerry with its distinctive white face and black markings round its nose and eyes, and by the native Clun, first written about in 1837.

In Montgomery the key to the vegetation is the lack of lime. The county is noted for the beauty of its oaks, especially fine in the park of Powys Castle. In spring primroses abound in the hedgerows, and in summer, honeysuckle.

By contrast, a quite different community exists on the poorer, more acid soils of the Clwydians and Black Mountains. Rampant bracken of the lower slopes gives way to seas of purple heath, a fine sight in the Clwydians in late summer. Only in the higher Black Mountains, though, does the footpath continue upwards to moor where bilberry (*Vaccinium myrtillus*) dominates, and finally, on the deep peat, to bleak and desolate moors of cottongrass (*Eriophorum vaginatum*).

In the south-east corner of the Black Mountains the very occasional Red Grouse that may be found here are the remnant of Britain's most southerly indigenous population of that bird. Other species of these moors include the Black Grouse and the Curlew.

For the last miles to the sea the underlying limestone has a characteristic fauna and flora. In the vicinity of Dyserth that eighteenth-century traveller, the Reverend W. Bingley, remarking on the richness of the flora, claims to have found the rare Spiked Speedwell (*Veronica spicata*), more usually associated with East Anglia's dry grasslands, the locally found Blood-red Geranium (*Geranium sanguineum*) and the rock-rose (*Cistus helianthemum*).

Each year changes occur in different parts of the Border and species disappear or change their habits. A wide range of plants, animals and insects remains, and each area has its special attractions at particular times of year. I prefer, for instance, the Wye Valley in spring for its bluebell woods, and before the leaves become too dense to obscure views over the valley; and the Clwydians in late summer for their heather, and in autumn for the russet of the bracken. Whenever you choose to follow the Dyke you will find something in the wild life of interest and appeal.

Sedbury cliffs to Monmouth: the Wye Valley

*Blessed is the eye
'Twixt the Severn and Wye*

Thomas Fuller: *Gnomologia*

To the present-day traveller along the first mile of the Dyke the old rhyme would seem scarcely appropriate. For, after the fine prospect from the end of the Dyke across the Severn Estuary, the path takes a complicated course through the urban fringe sprawl on the Beachley Peninsula. Fortunately, from Chepstow northwards, things improve and for the next 16 miles to Monmouth comes one of the finest sections of the whole route along the wooded slopes of the Wye Valley where indeed "blessed *is* the eye".

To reach the start of the path you may take the Beachley bus from Chepstow to Buttington Tump and follow the footpath in reverse. Here, out beyond the sprawl of modern development, at the point where Offa's Dyke reaches the sea, the path begins by a solitary grey boulder. To west and south the land falls steeply away, and to the east, 100 feet below a tree-grown cliff, lie the wide and dangerous waters of the Severn, narrowing southwards to the sweep of the M4 Motorway bridge, before finally river becomes sea. Landwards the view takes in nearly all the low-lying Beachley Peninsula, often shrouded in mist, to the meeting of the Severn and Wye.

If you continue down the slope to the south-west it is possible to walk out on to the saltmarsh, almost to the water's edge, and there look up to the cliffs and the point where Offa's Dyke finishes and your journey begins.

Back on the cliff top you descend along the line of an overgrown though massive section of Dyke, following it to the B4228 at the prominent piece of Dyke known as Buttington Tump, and the beginning of the mile of sprawl where the path runs by a much defiled earthwork through piecemeal urban fringe development. For the next four miles there is some complicated route finding (follow the map closely) before the path finally rejoins the Dyke on Tidenham Chase. 21

Through the estate of Pennsylvania Village, set blatantly on the Dyke, the path takes you on to lower ground: Tallard's Marsh, a creek negotiable by small boats as recently as the 1850s. Where the sewage works is today, there used to be a saw mill.

The path turns north through a modern housing estate, beside limestone crags that fall steeply to the Wye, and back to the B4228 which you follow across a railway cutting. Before long the path continues in a pleasant canyon between high limestone walls, to a junction of walled paths. Here you may either continue uphill along the route of the Dyke Path or turn down to Rennie's white iron bridge and cross over to Chepstow on the Gwent side of the Wye.

Chepstow is the obvious place to stay before setting out along the path. There is a variety of accommodation and a reasonably wide selection of shops. It is also on the railway from Gloucester to Cardiff. Within its walls the town still retains its medieval street pattern. From the castle the main street, congested despite (or perhaps because of) the M4, climbs steeply through Beaufort Square towards the fortified gateway.

At one time Chepstow ("market place") was a trading centre of some importance. Edward Davies in the eighteenth century says of it:

"Corn, cider, timber are exported hence,
And ships are built for traffic and defence:
The Irish trade increases ev'ry day,
And ships from Chepstow visit Dublin Bay."

And Defoe found it "a town of very good trade . . . to this town ships of a good burthen may come up, and the tide here runs with the same impetuous current at Bristol; the flood rising from six fathom and a half at Chepstow Bridge".

The castle, founded by William Fitzosbern, who led the first Norman assault on Wales, was the first Norman stronghold to be built on Welsh soil. It was strategically placed at the point where the main route into South Wales crossed the Wye, and overlooked the harbour and route by which supplies could be brought from Bristol.

After several changes of ownership, both private and Crown, the castle came, in 1189, under William Marshall. During the succeeding decades it was much added to and strengthened. The present castle remains essentially as it was in the thirteenth century under Roger Bigod, third earl of that name. Viewed from the Gloucestershire bank of the Wye, the sight is most impressive, the castle seeming to grow from the limestone cliffs that rise sheer from the river.

Between Monmouth and Chepstow the Wye follows a winding, at times spectacular, course along the edge of the Forest of Dean. The Wye in this section is a classic example of a rejuvenated river where successive periods of downcutting have occurred, with short phases when the river built up a narrow flood plain, and when the remarkable flat spurs of land such as the Lancaut Peninsula were formed. It is this combination of gorge and cliff, lower-lying spurs, and extensive woodland on the steep valley sides which is an obvious tourist attraction. But you won't meet many people as you follow the Dyke on its winding course through the woods high above the river and road.

22   Continuing northwards the Dyke Path soon turns into a rising field,

Monnow Bridge

crossing the line of the Roman road from Glevum (Gloucester) to Venta Silurum (Caerwent) as it descends to the old Striguil Bridge over the Wye. Beyond the remains of the sixteenth-century Tutshill look out tower things improve as you enter pleasant parklike surroundings. Although the path is running close to the Wye in this stretch views are eastwards to the Severn across gently sloping land, except for an all-too-brief section near Broadrock where you suddenly emerge on the very edge of a deeply quarried cliff above the Wye, and follow a fenced path past the quarry rim to the Wintour's Leap viewpoint.

It was to Sir John Wintour that Charles I leased the whole of the Forest of Dean. At one time, it is said, he had 500 axemen at work, but Cromwell soon put a stop to this drastic felling. Wintour is best remembered in the (apocryphal?) story telling of his escape from an attack by Parliamentarian troops on Beachley by leaping his horse over the 200-foot cliff now called after him. From the viewpoint you can look down-river to Chepstow on the skyline and below to the Lancaut Peninsula almost encircled by a loop of the river, beneath the great Wynd Cliff, and where there is one farm, one small ruined church, and one parish.

There follows a mile of road, woodland, field and more road before you turn off eastward beyond Dennel Hill House, and enter the magnificent woodlands that cover the steep sides of the Wye Valley, forming the western edges of the Forest of Dean.

In early times the Forest almost covered the whole triangle of land between the Severn and Wye, the area occupied by the Silures. These were the first people to mine the ore found in the Forest. During the Middle Ages there was drastic felling of trees because of the demand for charcoal for fuel in the forges, continuing through to the 23

Llanthony Priory

seventeenth century when Wintour felled as many as 20,000 trees. In the Forest of Dean so famous were the oaks that, according to John Evelyn, the commanders of the Spanish Armada were given special instructions to destroy this invaluable source of timber.

A short distance from Dennel Hill you rejoin a modest Dyke contouring the slopes some 600 feet above the river. For some way now the route follows the Dyke through the upper edges of the badger woods, along the west side of Tidenham Chase, through Worgan's Wood, angling sharply north along the Shorn Cliff. For much of the year views through the trees are limited, until you suddenly arrive at the superb viewpoint at the Devil's Pulpit. You look down from the Dyke across the outcropping platform rock to Tintern Abbey in its beautiful valley setting, a strangely evocative landscape scene, calling to mind Wordsworth's famous lines written a few miles above Tintern. Edward Davies recalled a less idyllic scene from the time when there was an ironworks at Tintern itself:

> "Black forges smoke and noisy hammers beat,
> Where sooty cyclops, puffing, drink and sweat;
> Confront the curling flames, nor back retire,
> But live like salamanders in the fire."

It was to Tintern that Stephen Harding of Sherborne, the true founder of the Cistercians, came in 1131. The abbey's founder was Walter de Clare. The original building was probably modest in concept; and it was not until 1274 that the new work was started, to be dedicated 14 years later. In those days so dense were the woods that the monks who built the abbey laboured in a jungle of trees. So complete was their isolation that the Devil is said to have preached to them from the Pulpit rock, to lure them back to worldliness. Whether he achieved his purpose is not known; suffice it to say that at the Dissolution there were a mere dozen monks left at the abbey.

Beyond the Devil's Pulpit the Dyke swings round the head of a combe where a path leads down to Tintern through the woods of Passage Grove; but you keep with the Dyke as it contours the valley side. The going along the Dyke is at times rough, especially when you are walking on the uneven rocky bank of the work, and where the stumps of cleared undergrowth are a hazard. On lower slopes the main hazards are mud and hard-packed clay which, when wet, becomes extremely slippery.

On emerging from the woods on Madgett Hill there is a choice of routes. Either you can follow the line of an intermittent Dyke along walled and hedged tracks, through the patchwork of small fields and scattered houses on St Briavels Common, or you can turn downhill to Brockweir and follow the banks of the Wye to Bigsweir where the alternatives meet. If you are intending to stay at St Briavels then you will probably prefer to take the "Dyke" alternative. Otherwise the "Wye" alternative is better in that this is the only time between Chepstow and Monmouth when you will have a chance to see the river at close quarters; and it is a pleasant change to come down from the woods and Dyke for a while.

St Briavels, one and a half miles off route, is a forest village with a Norman church and the remains of a castle that became a debtors' prison, once described as having "only one window, which is one foot wide . . . and does not open". The castle is now a Youth Hostel. In the Middle Ages St Briavels was a busy little town, an administrative centre for the Forest of Dean, and iron smelting went on there. It was not everyone who could mine the ore of the Forest Crown lands, the right to do so being long restricted to the so-called Freeminers, men aged over 21, born in the hundred of St Briavels, and who had worked for at least a year and a day in the mines. Today St Briavels is a quiet village, away from the main tourist traffic of the Wye Valley.

If you take the Wye alternative a wide track leads down to the hamlet of Brockweir. If you left the route earlier to visit Tintern you may pick it up again here by following paths on the east side of and parallel to the Wye. The path now turns north with the river bank and leads through level meadows backed by wooded slopes. You pass Coed-Ithel Weir where the woods come down to the water's edge and soon come to the normal tidal limit of the Wye at Llandogo, with its houses rising one above another on the steep western bank. The village is named after St Oudoceus, to whom a sixth-century prince granted land and fisheries equal in extent to that covered by the deer he had been hunting that day. The saint wanted the lands for a monastery, but of such there is no trace.

Soon you join a track which leads to Bigsweir House. In summer the next few yards of path are remarkably tropical as you plunge through a tunnel of *Polygonum cuspidatum* (the Japanese Polygonum), a giant plant growing as high as eight or nine feet. The alternative routes are close together here, the one hugging the river bank, the other descending through meadows from St Briavels Common. Both cross the Mork Brook and emerge, a few yards apart, on the A466.

In this vicinity the wooded valley side makes a wide arc away from 25 the present course of the river, evidence that at one time the Wye flowed here in a meander loop, severed as it cut down into its bed. The Mork Brook marks one side of the loop, and its smaller branch to the south the other.

Half a mile of road walking from Bigsweir Bridge and the path is once more following the Dyke, through woods and fields on Highbury Plain, at times with yews of giant size growing on the earthwork. Emerging from the woods by abandoned Highbury Farm you look at last towards the opening out of the valley at Monmouth with the Kymin, the next hill on route, beyond.

On the narrow strip of land between river and valley side you come to the small industrial settlement of Lower Redbrook, where the downstream branch of a second abandoned meander loop comes in from the south-east. Soon you leave the main road and enter the side valley containing the scattered houses of Upper Redbrook, and where the other arm of the meander once flowed. Both valleys now contain streams which have considerably deepened the original course of the Wye. When the iron industry came to the area these streams were used to drive the bellows and forge hammers.

Redbrook's interest lies in its geography and industrial archaeology, not in its visual attractions, though you may be interested in the limited accommodation there. At Redbrook the Dyke peters out, and for many miles now the long-distance path detours away from its line. On the final stretch to Monmouth the climb to the Kymin, on a rough, sunken track, is long and tedious, especially if your day began at Chepstow. You will encounter other tracks like this in the next day or so. The track at last gives way to steadily rising fields, and soon you emerge from a small plantation at the National Trust property with its curious Naval Temple and Round House, and one of the most far-flung views on the whole walk, the view which Nelson, visiting the hill in 1802, described as one of the finest he had seen. On clear days you look in the far distance for a first glimpse of the Black Mountains.

The Kymin's history as a viewpoint and place of recreation goes back to 1793 when the "first gentlemen in Monmouth" decided to build the pavilion known as the Round House in which to hold weekly meetings. The whimsical Naval Temple which followed was built in 1800 to perpetuate the names of some of the distinguished admirals of the latter half of the eighteenth century. You leave the Kymin through a cleft in some rocks on the north-west side, following the path to the north of the scattered houses and chalets on the side of the hill, descending rapidly by field, wood and road to the frayed edges of Monmouth, over the Wye, under the fast A40, and into the pleasant, unassuming centre of the town.

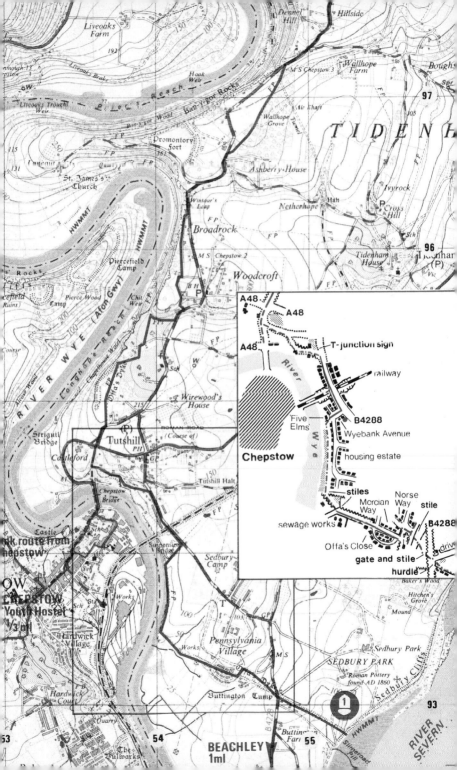

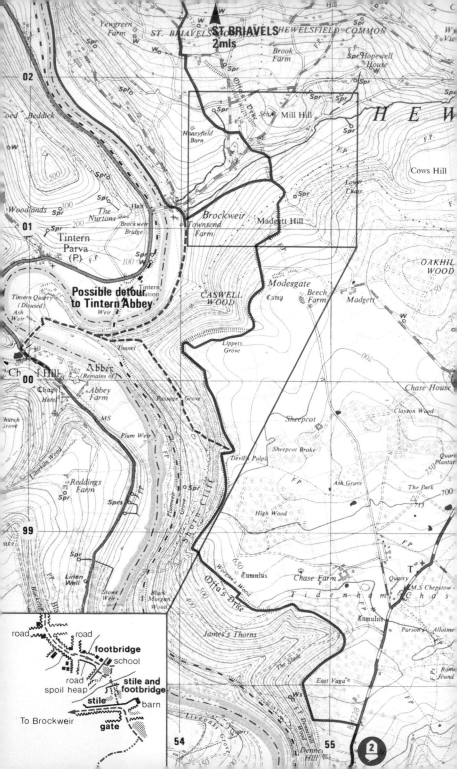

ST. BRIAVELS
2mls

Possible detour to Tintern Abbey

road — road
footbridge
school
road
spoil heap
stile and footbridge
stile
barn
gate
To Brockweir

②

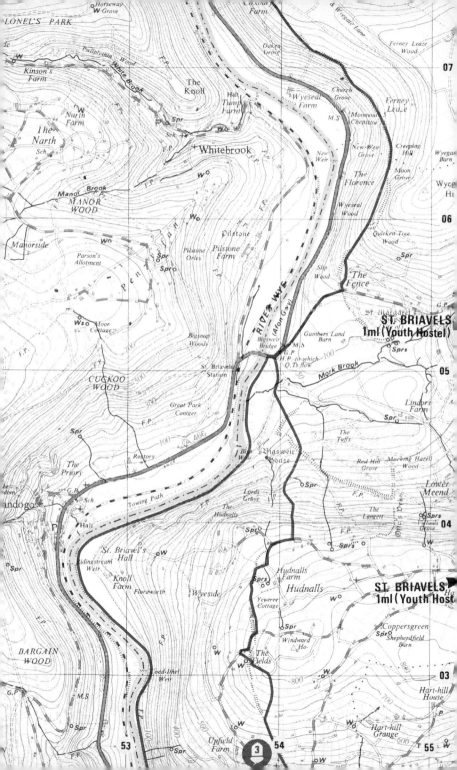

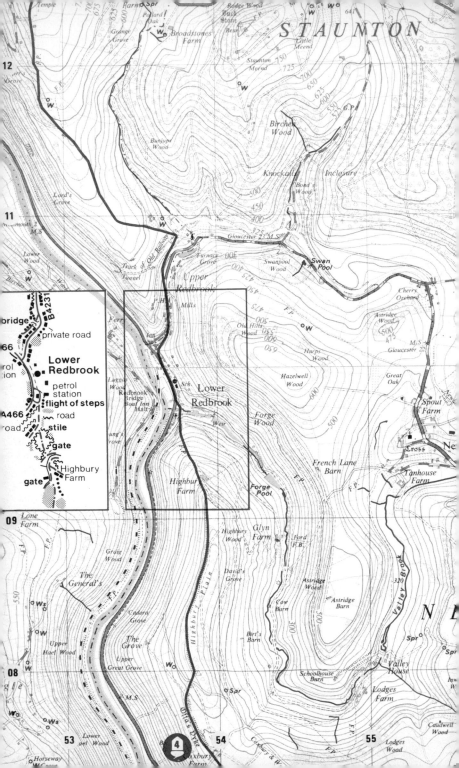

STAUNTON

Lower Redbrook

- B4231
- private road
- petrol station
- flight of steps
- road
- stile
- gate
- Highbury Farm
- gate

A466

Lower Redbrook

Highbury Farm

Redbrook Bridge Boat Inn Halt

Upper Redbrook

Knockalls Inclosure

Birchen Wood

Swan Pool

Swanpool Wood

Bond's Wood

Turnace Grove

Hazelwell Wood

Great Oak

Cherry Orchard

Astridge Wood

Spout Farm

Cross

Tanhouse Farm

Forge Wood

Weir

French Lane Barn

Forge Pool

Glyn Farm

Highbury Wood

Ford F.B.

Astridge Wood

Astridge Barn

Valley House

Lodges Farm

Lone Farm

Craig Wood

The General's

Cadora Grove

The Grove

Upper Hael Wood

Upper Great Grove

David's Grove

Cow Barn

Birt's Barn

Schoolhouse Barn

Lodges Wood

Caudwell Wood

Highbury Plain

Offa's Dyke

Valley Brook

12

11

09

08

53   54   55

4

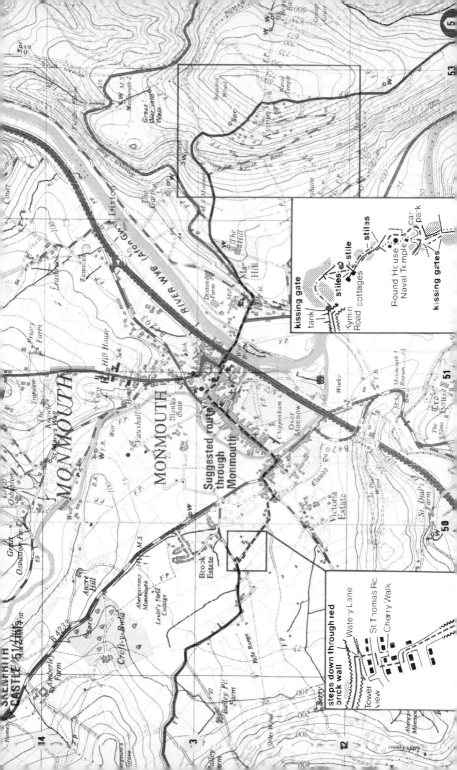

Monmouth to Pandy: the Monmouthshire lowlands

... got to Monmouth to dinner through a rugged ... country; and from thence through a flat fertile country.

Defoe: *Journey through England by a Gentleman*

The confluence of Wye and Monnow was an obvious place for a town to develop after the Norman incursion into the Border. Not only did the rivers provide excellent natural defence, but the land between was high enough to be free from flooding. Monmouth grew round the church and castle, and by the fourteenth century it was a walled town and chartered borough. Like Chepstow its original street pattern survives, though only a mound now remains of the castle, Henry V's birthplace in 1387. The broad street that runs down from Agincourt Square, the old market place, to the famous thirteenth-century fortified bridge, unique in this country, is where, in Norman times, were miasmal and often flooded marshes.

Monmouth is the birthplace of Geoffrey of Monmouth, the Benedictine monk who wrote the interesting if inaccurate *History of the Kings of Britain*. As at Chepstow you will find a suitably wide range of shops, eating places, and accommodation. If you can spend a little time in Monmouth the Nelson Museum is well worth a visit.

The landscape over the next 16 miles to Pandy, though not exceptional, can provide a pleasant walk if the weather is fine. In bad weather the lush pastures can make the going underfoot at least as wet as the wilder moorland stretches of the route. This was one of the last sections of the walk to be cleared and waymarked, and as recently as 1970 the rights of way often existed in theory only.

You leave Monmouth by the Monnow Bridge and enter the later suburb of Over Monnow, once famous for its hat-making. "If your Majesties is rememb'red of it," says Fluellen in *Henry V,* "the Welshmen did good service in a garden where leeks did grow, wearing leeks in their Monmouth caps." Once the custom of covering the head with the hood of one's cloak died out, hat making became a business of considerable importance. But it was not permissible to wear any hat one pleased, and it was not uncommon in the sixteenth century for fines to be levied on those wearing hats beyond their stations in life.

From the Wonastow Road the path lies through housing estates to Watery Lane on the way to Bailey Pit Farms. Where the lane becomes a track you turn right through a gateway into a field beside a deeply sunken old track where a watercourse has long disputed the right of way, following the path through overgrown pastures and scrubby woodland in the vicinity of the derelict Upper Bailey Pit Farm. You enter the mixed woods and plantations of King's Wood, following clear paths and tracks to the Trothy (Troddi) Valley at the farms at Hendre.

This is an undulating landscape, little by little rising towards the Black Mountains, and crossed by numerous small streams draining to the Trothy; a landscape of hedged fields, pastoral on the lower and wetter areas, tending to arable on the higher "plateaux" between the small valleys. The route takes you through pastures, passing the site of Grace Dieu, the Anglo-Norman abbey affiliated to Waverley Abbey, and founded in 1226 by John de Monmouth; and soon to the isolated medieval church of Llanvihangel-Ystern-Llewern, attractively set on rising ground among trees. The church is said to have been founded by Ynyr, king of Gwent, on the place where he reached firm ground after stumbling into a marsh.

A succession of fields and road (perhaps too much road) leads unerringly to the bar in the "Hostry Inn" at Llantilio Crossenny. There has been a "Hostry Inn" here since 1459, though after a murder, exactly 400 years later, it was closed until 1900. The present building is attractively symmetrical, with a curious octagonal chimney above the front door. A few yards to the right of the point where the Dyke Path crosses the B4233, as you leave Llantilio, is the site of Hen Cwrt, the moated medieval mansion of Sir David Gam, knighted by Henry V at Agincourt.

At the large steading of Treadam you turn up a long mile of metalled farm lane to White Castle. The name, in Welsh Castell Gwyn, appears to have been in use, rather than the original name of Llantilio Castle, as early as the thirteenth century, and is a reference to the white plaster once coating the walls. Isolated on its commanding hill the castle looks west towards Ysgyryd Fawr, now very dominant in the landscape. White Castle, dating from around 1184–1185, is one of three that came into being in the twelfth century with the Norman advance beyond the Wye. The others are at Skenfrith and Grosmont, worth a visit if you are car-based.

Beyond White Castle there are one or two steep though short ascents as the headwaters of the Trothy are reached. The path descends fields to Caggle Street, crossing the Trothy for the last time, and climbs via a rutted lane before descending to the Full Brook. The way follows a pleasant grassy track through Little Pool Hall Farm, along nearly a mile of road, and past Old Court Farm, a Jacobean house once owned by Sir William Morgan who was in charge of artillery in Cromwell's army. Captain Morgan, the buccaneer, from the same family and one-time Governor of Jamaica, is buried in the churchyard at Llangattock-lingoed hamlet, a quarter-mile farther along the footpath. "The Hunter's Moon" at Llangattock, formerly "The Carpenters' Arms", is a grey stone inn, built in 1217 and still in its original state.

After a further mile of walking through pastures and along lanes you top the long ridge, running from Ysgyryd Fawr to Grosmont, that divides the Trothy from the Honddu and Monnow Valleys. Ahead the great open Hatterrall Ridge sweeps up from the fields in the valley, and stretches away into the distance. You have suddenly come from a landscape of small scale to a landscape of vast scale: the contrast is impressive, the view superb.

The path makes a rapid descent across fields to the busy A465 opposite the "Lancaster Arms". There is a choice of accommodation at Pandy to the right, or at Llanvihangel-Crucorney to the left. Pandy exists as a mere scattering of houses along the main road, but there is a surprisingly good range of accommodation to choose from, including farms, a hotel, and three inns. The name means "fulling mill", for one existed here at one time driven by the Honddu.

Llanvihangel-Crucorney, at the entrance to Cwm Ewyas, and in the shadow of Ysgyryd Fawr, is best known for its fine Elizabethan gabled house, Llanfihangel Court, which has a front dating from 1559. The house is open to the public. The "Skirrid Mountain Inn", built of local stone, goes even further back to medieval times. Modern-looking though it may be, it was built in 1110. The inn has a beautifully carved wooden staircase leading to the courtroom used by Judge Jeffreys when he was on circuit. A cross-beam below the stairs has rope marks worn on it where cattle-thieves were hanged.

Rhydspence Inn

King's Wood

plantations

fork right at head of dell

wicket gate
by field
gate

shed

stile

scrub
woodland

gap

Upper
Bailey Pit
Farm

6

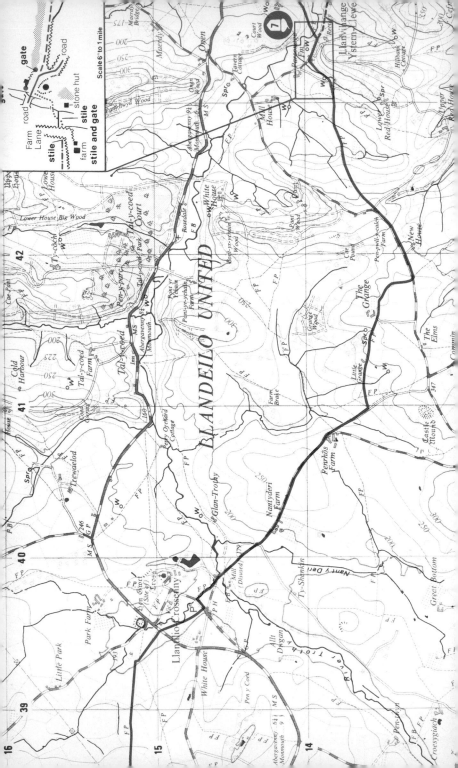

Pandy to Hay-on-Wye: the Black Mountains

Under the cloudless blue and glorious sunshine the Abbey looked happy and peaceful. . . . How different from the first day that I pilgrimaged down the Vale of Ewyas under a gloomy sky, the heavy mist wreathing along the hillsides cowling the mountain tops. . . .

Kilvert's Diary

The next 17 miles to Hay provide some of the finest open hill walking on the Offa's Dyke Path, along the Hatterrall Ridge, the easternmost of the high ridges of the Black Mountains, falling away on one side to the Olchon Valley, and on the other to the deeply entrenched valley of the Honddu, Cwm Ewyas.

Meeting the full force of the rain-bearing south-westerlies, the Black Mountains are the wettest area along the whole Border, with a rainfall of nearly 60″ a year. Often louring cloud hangs low over these mountains, or lashing rain sweeps their tops when surrounding areas are in sun. Then indeed these mountains, sombre and brooding, well merit their name.

If the weather looks doubtful you would do well to consider the wisdom of making for the tops, rather than keeping to a valley route to Hay. This may not be "doing the path", but it could prove safer. It is a good plan to spend two days over the Black Mountains, remembering, however, that you will have to make the exceptionally steep descent to the Olchon or Honddu Valleys to find accommodation and face the scramble back the following morning. But by breaking your journey you will find time to make the detour to the ruins of Llanthony Priory on the Honddu side of the ridge, and to explore Hay at the end of the second day's walk.

An Offa's Dyke sign by the "Lancaster Arms" on the A465 points the way across a field to the wooded hollow where the Honddu flows northwards. At one time this river, leaving Cwm Ewyas, continued to flow south towards Abergavenny, down the valley now occupied by the Gavenni River. After the Ice Ages, as the ice retreated, leaving behind a moraine some 150 feet high that effectively blocked the valley, the Honddu was diverted in a circuitous loop north-west to join the Monnow which, once flowing south to join the Honddu, now flows north-east through a narrow gorge-like valley.

The way leads uphill over the Hereford–Abergavenny railway, past a castle motte in its cluster of pines near the farm at Tre-fedw, and on via lane and field path to a col where the view opens out towards the Sugar Loaf and other southern hills of the Black Mountains. You leave the lane on its descent back to Pandy where a track goes off on the left, climbing soon through rampant bracken towards a conspicuous clump of pines at Pen-twyn, and the first of the several Iron Age hill forts *en route*.

Now the way runs clear for several miles along the back of the Hatterrall Hill ridge, through seas of heather and bilberry. Besides being splendid walking country the ridges of the Black Mountains have become popular with pony trekkers during the last 20 years, and you will be unlucky not to see groups of Welsh ponies and cobs grazing somewhere on these high tops.

The track continues over the broad back of the hill, down to a narrowing of the ridge as views open out to the west, to distant heights, and into the beautiful and sequestered Honddu Valley. Eastwards a more wide-ranging view takes in a broad sweep of countryside: back towards Ysgyryd Fawr and the low hills of Gwent, ahead over the patchwork of the undulating Plain of Hereford. In the Olchon Valley, at the foot of the rounded hill of Mynydd Merddin, Longtown's castle keep on its mound by the river is conspicuous. On a clear day, 15 miles away, Hereford appears as a brush stroke of white in the landscape, and the Malverns, twice that distance away, form a distinctive profile on the horizon.

By Black Daren, where the ridge widens once again westward to the Loxidge Tump, the track has dwindled to a path (a torrent in wet weather). If you keep to the main path you will find yourself bearing too far west, for the Dyke Path keeps more north-westerly, over the back of the broad hill. The exact point to leave the Loxidge path is not clear, the maze of sheeptracks here only serving to confuse.

Llanthony Priory is directly below "in the deep Vale of Ewyas" which, as the twelfth-century itinerant Giraldus Cambrensis described it, "is about an arrow shot broad". The priory he found "not unhandsomely constructed". It is, in fact, well worth a detour. The route via the Loxidge Tump is shown on map No. 11 on page 44. You come to the priory ruins in a beautiful setting of meadows and groves of chestnut planted by the poet Landor when he lived here. It is said that St David settled at Llanthony during his travels through Wales in the sixth century, establishing the llan. It is unlikely he stayed long, but Llanthony's special claim to fame is that St David supposedly ate the leeks here that were to become the Welsh badge.

The priory was founded in 1107 by the powerful Marcher lord William de Lacy at the place where, on a deer hunt, he is said to have forsaken ambition and decided to devote his life to the service of God. As a result of Welsh raids the monks sought refuge with the bishop of Hereford, only a few returning to the priory. From 1300 the priory flourished once more, but by 1376 it was in a poor state of repair. Owain Glyndŵr burned it in about 1400; by 1481 only four canons and a prior remained; and the end came with the Dissolution by Henry VIII.

In 1807 the estate was bought by Walter Landor for £20,000. But he quarrelled with the local people, and finding it an "ungenial clime" left Llanthony in the hands of trustees. The remains of the poet's house lie at Siarpal in the cwm formed by the Hatterrall Ridge and the Loxidge Tump. The priory is now in the care of the Department of the Environment.

Four miles farther up-valley at Capel-y-ffin are the remains of another monastery, founded in 1870 by the Rev. J. L. Lyne (Father Ignatius) for the Benedictines. Soon after his death in 1908 the community ceased to exist, and the church is now a ruin. In the 1920s, though, the sculptor Eric Gill lived at the monastery for four years, and the house has remained in his family ever since. Besides the Catholic church at tiny Capel-y-ffin are a Baptist and an Anglican chapel. Just over a mile farther on towards the Gospel Pass is the Youth Hostel.

Back on the Dyke Path, from Black Daren northwards the way trends very gradually towards the unmarked summit of the ridge, and of the path, at 2,306 feet, on a broad and bleak nameless plateau of peat. The Olchon Valley to the east deepens as the great rocky ridge of the Cat's Back arches up towards Black Hill, laying bare the successive strata of Old Red Sandstone. The surrounding landscape becomes wild and remote, a place to avoid in mist and rain. A sinister legend tells of the Old Lady of the Black Mountains, said to appear at night or in mist in the form of an old woman with a pot or wooden cane in her hand, and who, going before a wayfarer, will cause him to lose his way. A friendlier spectre, said to appear to travellers lost in the mountains between Llanthony and Longtown, is of a man who will guide them to the nearest road before disappearing.

Ways down to the Olchon Valley between Black Daren and the valley head are hard to find through the crags (tarenni, hence Daren), the only relatively safe and easy ways down being via the steep "rhiws", old man-made gullies up which sheep were driven to the summer pastures, and which exist throughout the Daren slopes. But they are hard to locate from the ridge top.

Occasional posts which mark out the course of the path as it continues its peaty way tend to tilt and fall in the soft ground. The path has become far more erratic and there are more undulations than would appear from the map. Eventually you reach a short and steep descent by the Llech y Lladron, a short mile from Pen y Beacon. The official route, preferable in bad weather, angles down the east side of the moor to join the Gospel Pass road below the beacon. You may prefer to follow the waymarked alternative along the top of the ridge to the beacon itself. For most of the year this path to the bluff exists as a continuous ribbon of water, threading its way through a series of boggy pools and over soft ground, and on one of the most exposed sections of the crossing to Hay. From Kilvert's description the scene can have changed little in the past hundred years:

> "Soon we were at the top, which was covered with peat bog and black and yellow coarse rushy grass and reed. Here and there were pools and holes filled with black peat waters.... The mountains were very silent and desolate. No human being in sight, not a tree."

At Pen y Beacon (or Hay Bluff) you come to the steep north-west scarp of the Black Mountains, high above the middle Wye Valley. On this high and windswept bluff, on the very northern cornice of the 41 range, a wide-sweeping countryside stretches away almost to the limits of vision. Beyond the Wye, hidden from view, where the Dyke Path continues its journey, the Silurian hills of former Radnorshire rise to high grassy tops or to higher open hill common. In the distance are the outlines of the Mynydd Eppynt, and the Radnor Forest.

Dropping down over the cornice of Brownstones you aim between two deep gullies, and follow paths across easier ground to join the Gospel Pass road on its way from the Honddu Valley. Between this road and Hay (some three miles) the official route is under review and the walker is recommended to use the line on the map. A succession of metalled lanes, tracks and paths leads past the prehistoric burial mound at Twyn y Beddau, via Cadwgan Farm and along the side of Cusop Dingle, on the steady descent to Hay.

At Hay there is an adequate choice of shops and also accommodation (of variable quality), but you may prefer to find out-of-town accommodation at a nearby farm or inn, such as the "Rhydspence", just over an hour's walk away in Hereford county. In a triangle bounded on two sides by main roads Hay forms a compact and sleepy town. A notice in one shop window seemed to sum this up: Early Closing — Tuesday, Wednesday, Friday and Saturday.

In Hay are the remains of two castles, both Norman. The mound of the earlier motte and bailey, built around 1100 by William de Braose, is beyond the medieval core of the town, near St Mary's Church. Legend has it that the castle was in fact built, not by William, but by his wife, Maud de St Valerie (Moll Walbee). She is said to have built it in one night, carrying the stones in her apron. A pebble that dropped into her shoe she is reputed to have thrown into Llowes churchyard, three miles away. The "pebble" measures nine feet in length and one foot in thickness!

The later castle seems to have been destroyed by King John in 1215, and burnt by Llywelyn ap Iorwerth in 1231, though it was apparently still in use when Henry III rebuilt it in about 1233. In 1236 the town walls were built, and by 1298 a compact town had grown within them. The castle was captured and changed hands several times in the succeeding decades, so that John Leland in the sixteenth century found Hay to show "the token of a right strong Waulle having in Hit iii Gates and a Posterne. Ther is also a Castel the which sumtime hath bene right stately".

The seventeenth-century Jacobean castle incorporated into this castle is now owned by Mr. R. Booth who runs the remarkable second-hand book business in the town. Apart from the castle itself, where rarer books are kept, many buildings have become book stores. The collection is claimed to be the largest in the world, and it is worth setting aside time to explore some at least of the bookshops. But avoid the temptation to overload your rucksack with great tomes. There is some strenuous walking ahead.

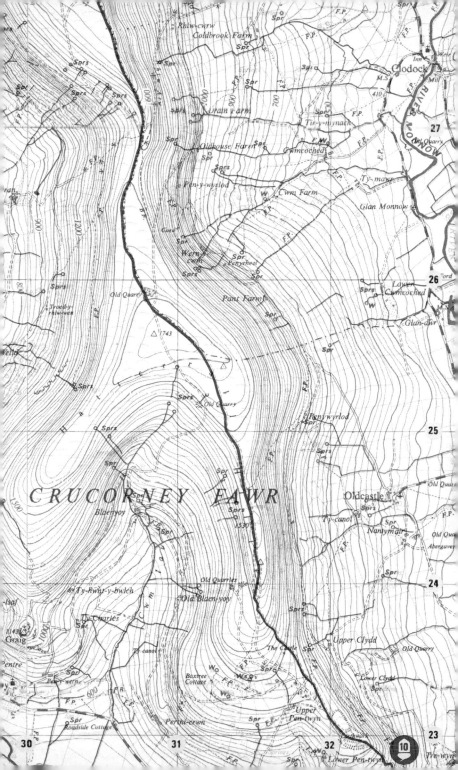

Possible detour to Llanthony Priory

Waymarked alternative

Recommended bad weather route from the Olchon Valley

Recommended bad weather route from Capel-y-ffin

CRASWA

L Y N F A C H

College Farm

Fidler's Farm

Probert's Farm

Old Gospel Ho

Valley Garth

Black Hill
2102 △

Olchon

Ford
Blaen-Olchon

Tow Hous

Firs Farm

The Place

Rhyd-l2s

Arthurys v

Spr

Pencelley

Spr

Olchon Co
Farm

2091 △ B.S

Spr

Spr

Ty-bach

Sprs

Ford
Brychen

Sprs

Trwyn-tal

Pen-y-maes

Capel-y-ffin

Monastery

Blaenau

Sprs

Spr

B.S

Spr

Sprs

Sprs

Nant Hywel

Nant yr Annell

2306

Daren

36

35

34

33

32

25

26

27

12

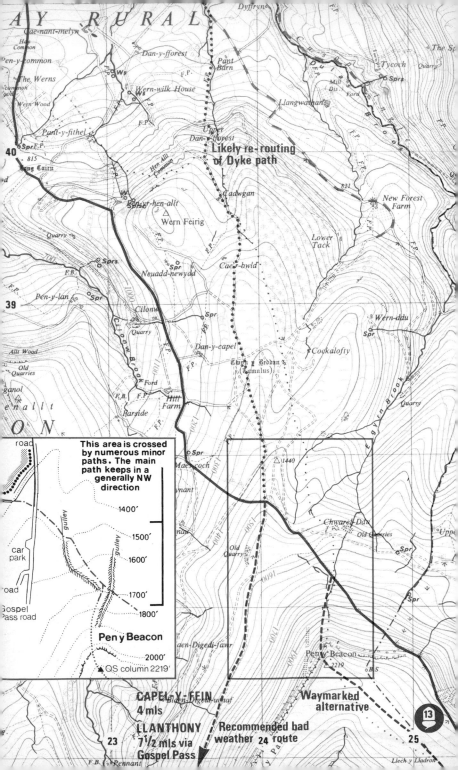

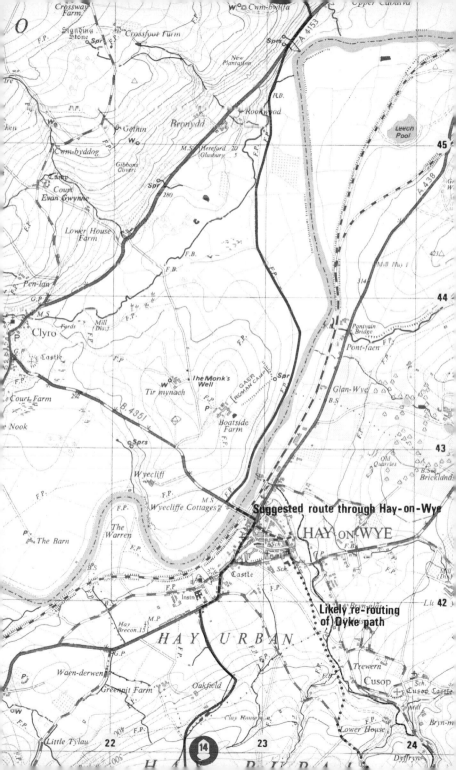

Suggested route through Hay-on-Wye

HAY on WYE

Likely re-routing of Dyke path

HAY URBAN

45

44

43

42

22   **14**   23   24

Hay-on-Wye to Knighton: the Radnorshire hills

No man ought to be in the government of this land who does not spend three months every year in such country as this.

George Bernard Shaw on Radnorshire

The next 40 miles to the lowlands around Montgomery through the Radnorshire hills and Clun district lie across the ancient outlying territory of Powys known as Rhwng Gwy a Hafren (between Wye and Severn). The constant ups and downs of this broken hill country provide the most strenuous walking on the Offa's Dyke Path. Although Mercian influence was strong in this part of the Border, this is essentially a countryside of dispersed habitation in the Welsh tradition. Much of the walk is through some of the quietest and most beautiful country along the Border.

Leaving Hay *en route* for Knighton you cross over the Wye into Kilvert country. A mile along the road lies Clyro where Francis Kilvert was curate from 1865–1872 and where, in 1870, he began his famous diary, describing vividly both the way of life in the area and much of the surrounding landscape. To anyone familiar with the diary the walk to Newchurch will be imbued with a particular interest.

The way does not continue to Clyro, however, but follows the Wye north-eastwards through wide level pastures, passing quite near to the large Roman marching camp at Boatside, upfield and west of the path. The camp, of which little remains, was evacuated before the end of the first hundred years of Roman occupation, and is the only evidence of such occupation in the Hay area.

The Herefords (including the occasional bull) that graze these pastures and the Border country ahead are said to be docile enough, and my experience has been that these cattle invariably turn a blind eye. Before long the A4153 is reached and followed for a short quarter-mile towards Rhydspence before an Offa's Dyke Path sign points the way up a steep lane on the left. The black and white timbered "Rhydspence Inn" lies a further mile along the road, just over the Border. Dating from the fourteenth century, it is reputed to be one of the oldest inns in Hereford county. It lies on an old drove road from Erwood to Hereford, and one from near Builth via Glascwm, and Newchurch to Hereford, and when droving was at its height in the eighteenth century was one of the drovers' stopping places.

Rising pastures soon climb beside the wooded slopes of Bettws Dingle. The way continues as a track through a plantation and out to a road that follows the line of the old Erwood–Hereford drove road via Painscastle. Following this road northwards, superb views soon open out to the south and east, over the Wye Valley and the Black Mountains. Shortly, beyond a lane junction, as the route descends into a dell, and off to the right, lies the church of Bettws Clyro where Kilvert preached, called Royal in medieval documents (from Yr Heol) in reference to a Roman road in the parish.

Soon a green road leads pleasantly over the back of the Pen-twyn Camp hill. This is part of the drove road from Rhydspence to Newchurch. It continues as a metalled lane to the sheep pastures of Little Mountain where Kilvert came on 6 May 1870 to find the lapwings "wheeling about the hill by scores, hurtling and rustling with their wings . . . very much disturbed, anxious and jealous about their nests". You keep northwards over the flank of the hill on a clear track, passing Gilfach-yr-heol Farm on its right to join a metalled lane that leads to the tiny hamlet of Newchurch. Great House Farm (and post office) is a building of character, and a good example of a cruck frame. It dates from the fourteenth–fifteenth centuries.

You follow the road through the village and out to the short-cropped slopes of Disgwylfa Hill. In 1645, when Charles I came to Wales, he passed just to the west of the hill, stopping at Blaencerde Farm on its slopes for a drink of milk. Kilvert tells of one of his parishioners who had the jug "that the king once drank out of. . . . He had breakfast that day in Brecon, dined at Gwernyfed and slept at Harpton, passing through Newchurch". On the lane the train of horsemen, riding two abreast, stretched for over a mile.

Hergest's striding ridge becomes dominant ahead as you follow the way down from Disgwylfa Hill and back to enclosed land. After a crossing of damp pastures at over 1,000 feet above sea level a quiet lane leads into the attractive hamlet of Gladestry (boasting a shop and an inn).

Hergest Ridge begins immediately to the east of Gladestry. The climb, for the first half-mile on a fenced lane, eases as the open common is reached. Ahead lie three miles of first-class walking on a clear grassy track, at times a wide swath of short turf, across the broad back of the ridge through bracken and gorse. Wide views take in the Black Mountains, the knolls surrounding the Vale of Radnor, the Radnor Forest, and the Malverns 30 miles away. The Dyke Path, avoiding the summit of the ridge, swings due east, over a crossing track, part of the old racecourse when Kington held its races here after 1824. The Whet Stone here is a boulder reputed to go down to the water to drink every morning at cock-crow.

Gradually you descend to the intake fence and follow a road past the gardens of Hergest Croft, noted for their rhododendrons and azaleas, and the fine collection of trees from all parts of the world, on down to the main A44 on the outskirts of Kington.

Turning from the Dyke Path, a lane off to the right here leads to Hergest Court (now a farm), seat of the Vaughans, the main landowners in the area in the Middle Ages. One of the best known of

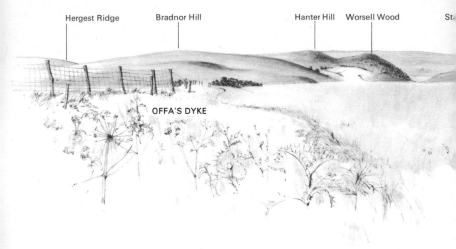

Hergest Ridge   Bradnor Hill   Hanter Hill   Worsell Wood   St

OFFA'S DYKE

the family, Thomas (Black) Vaughan, married Ellin Gethin (Ellen the
Terrible). She it was who went down to Tretower, west of Brecon, to
avenge the death of her brother killed by a kinsman. Dressed as a man
she shot him at an archery contest, escaping in the ensuing confusion.
Black Vaughan was killed during the Wars of the Roses at the Battle
of Banbury in 1469. His spirit could not rest. Twelve parsons
assembled to lay him. With them they had a silver snuff box and a
new-born child as a symbol of innocence. Each parson tried in turn,
but unsuccessfully, until one was left who persuaded Black Vaughan
to get into the snuff box with the baby. At his own request he was
buried in Hergest Pool where he must stay for a thousand years.

Throughout the fifteenth century Hergest Court was the centre of
Welsh culture. It was here that the Red and White Books of Hergest,
with their accounts of Welsh legend and folklore, were preserved.
Only *The Red Book of Hergest* now survives, housed in the Bodleian
Library in Oxford, where the Rev. John Jones translated it from Old to
Modern Welsh, and from which translation Lady Charlotte Guest
compiled the English version known as *The Mabinogion*.

You continue through the outskirts of Kington, passing St Mary's
Church on its knoll. The church has a Norman tower which was once
detached. The town, on the north of the Arrow, is predominantly
Victorian in character, though some fine Georgian houses still exist.
Kington may not be the pleasantest town on the long-distance path,
but if you set out from Hay in the morning it is a suitable end to a good
day's walk. There is accommodation in the town, and in neighbouring
farms, and a good choice of shops.

In the twelfth century Kington existed as a settlement clustered
around the church and castle. A later extension in the thirteenth
century was known as Kington in the Fields, and this is where the
present town grew up. The path does not, in fact, enter the main street
of Kington but turns away north by the ford at Back Brook, and up to

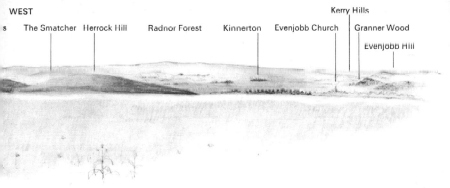

WEST   Kerry Hills

s   The Smatcher   Herrock Hill   Radnor Forest   Kinnerton   Evenjobb Church   Granner Wood

                                                                          Evenjobb Hill

The view from Rushock Hill

the open common and National Trust property of Bradnor Hill, site of the Kington races from the 1770s until they moved to Hergest Ridge. At over 1,200 feet, the golf course on the hill is the highest in England. If you are staying in the area and the weather is fine, a stroll to Bradnor Hill for the view at sunset is not to be missed.

Through enclosed pastures the path climbs on to Rushock Hill, 300 yards west of the Three Shepherds, three ancient yews that form a distinctive feature in the landscape from many miles around, and mark the point where the Dyke breasts the hill as it climbs back from the lowlands. Turning sharp west along its diminutive bank you follow it to the top of the hill at a sharp re-alignment, and so begin the descent to the Vale of Radnor, down the east side of Herrock Hill, away from the Dyke, to the B4362 at Lower Harpton.

Two miles farther west, at the foot of Old Radnor Hill, stands Old Radnor itself. Its church, at 840 feet above sea level, on a rocky eminence, contains what is probably the oldest font existing in Britain. Made from a megalithic stone the font has been in use since the eighth century. Three miles farther on is the medieval planned town of New Radnor, which succeeded Old Radnor in about 1250, but which lost its borough status in 1886. It was from New Radnor that Archbishop Baldwin and Giraldus Cambrensis began their preaching tour of Wales.

Across the Hindwell Valley you rejoin the line of the Dyke, turning up a track on the side of Burfa Hill with its huge crowning fort attributed to the Ordovices. Through the extensive farm of Burfa (note the cruck frame farmhouse) you come to a lane crossing and climb on to the Dyke, following its well-marked bank uphill, on an uneven path (hard going) through pastures and cornfields, above Evenjobb, through Granner Wood plantation, and round the head of Evenjobb Dingle. The Dyke, all the time commanding a westward prospect, follows easy gradients, in long straight stretches that,

The Black Mountains from above Bettws Dingle

switching backwards and forwards to avoid the ravines that run east and west from the main hill mass, bear witness to the sheer mastery of their engineer.

The descent to Yew Tree Farm begins. The Dyke, at first small-scale and sinuous, indicating that its course must originally have lain through woodland, reaches striking proportions on the middle slopes (originally open hill country). On the floor of the Lugg Valley where the Dyke is intermittent your way lies north-east, beside an old sunken track, now a watercourse, to Dolley Green, two miles from Presteigne, once the smallest county town in England and Wales.

On Furrow Hill a winding path brings you up to the Dyke once more, a very intermittent and diminutive affair, with the ditch on the east side, where it remains (apart from a short run on the hill above Knighton, and at Knighton itself) all the way to Cwm-sanaham Hill. From field to field your way runs beside the Dyke, only diverging from it once, midway between Furrow and Hawthorn Hills. The views throughout this stretch are very fine: Radnor Forest due west, the Kerry Hills further north; Herrock Hill is southward, and over 20 miles away the distant Black Mountains are in sight for the last time. Beyond the top of Hawthorn Hill the Dyke assumes a normal scale as you follow it through a succession of fields past the monument to Sir Richard Green-Price.

At the B4355 crossing a nineteenth-century stone, set on the bank of the Dyke, is the first of two such (the other being at Selattyn in Clwyd). The suspect date of 757 given for the Dyke's construction is the first year of Offa's reign.

After some road walking and a succession of fields the path enters the woods beside Knighton Golf Course and drops quickly to a housing estate on the edge of the town. A few minutes' walk brings you to the steep main street of Knighton.

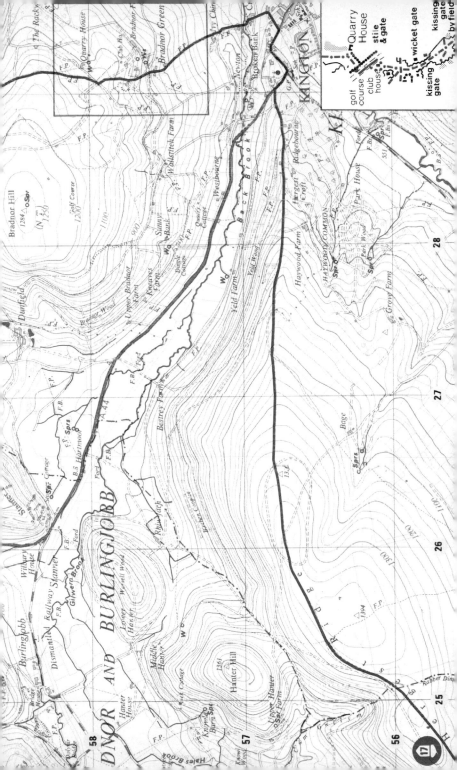

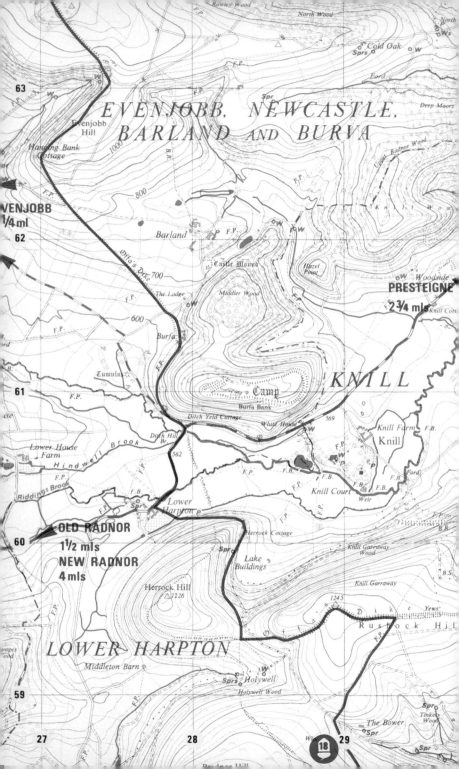

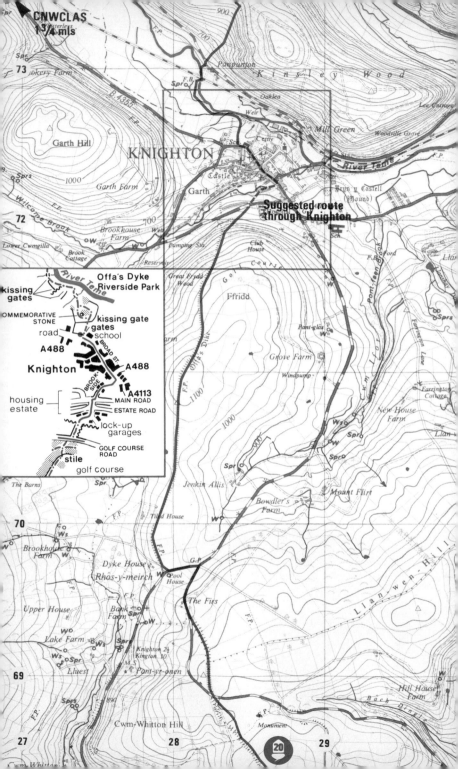

Knighton to Brompton Hall: the Clun hills

So great a work could hardly have been completed or even initiated until the Mercian realm came under the control of a man of exceptional competence, energy and power of organisation.

Sir Cyril Fox on Offa's Dyke

In the "V" of land between the Teme and the Wylcwm Brook a glacial ridge forms a prominent knoll. Across its flank, between the two rivers, Offa's Dyke formed the third side of a defensible triangle of land. As early, it is thought, as the Saxon period the beginnings of a town appeared here. Certainly the Welsh overran it in 1052, to such effect, it seems, that the site is recorded in the Domesday Book as unpopulated and a waste. The town that developed below the castle was granted to the Mortimers by Henry III. The castle appears to have been destroyed during the early part of the fifteenth century. In 1460 the town passed to Prince Edward (later Edward IV), when it became Crown property.

In the seventeenth century, with more settled times, Knighton continued to grow, with the development of the Swan Hotel and other buildings in the Town Clock Square. A major building phase in the early nineteenth century was associated with a prosperous agriculture and woollen industry, and a flourishing social life. The town has changed little since, though it has spread a little round the edges.

Knighton, with a population of a mere 2,500, is the largest town along the Offa's Dyke Path, apart from those at the coastal extremities. It is therefore appropriate that the Offa's Dyke Association and the Tref-y-clawdd "1970" Society should be based in this "capital" of the Dyke. In Knighton you will find accommodation and a wide range of shops.

You leave the town through the Offa's Dyke Park, passing the commemorative stone (by a well-preserved section of Dyke) that marks the official opening of the long-distance path. The path continues beside the Teme towards Panpunton Hill and the beginning of the Clun district of Salop.

This "remote outlying cantle wedged in between the Welsh mountains of Montgomeryshire and Radnorshire" covers some 90 square miles of rounded open hill country, cut by deep valleys. Today 59

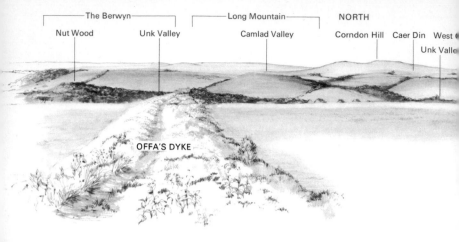

The Berwyn | Long Mountain | NORTH

Nut Wood   Unk Valley   Camlad Valley   Corndon Hill   Caer Din   West

Unk Valle

OFFA'S DYKE

this upland plateau is predominantly open pasture land divided up into extensive fenced enclosures. The more limited area known as the Clun Forest, rising to over 1,600 feet, forms the central core of this whole region. Originally, although much of the Clun district was probably heavily wooded, other parts were the rough moorland of today, where deer at one time roamed. Gradually demand for timber for houses and by charcoal burners denuded the area of woodland. While large areas are now being re-planted, it is with conifers rather than deciduous trees.

This was an area where Marcher lords struggled to extend their lordships westward. It seemed often more Welsh than English in character. Even today the area seems to have greater affinities with Wales. In this remote countryside the Dyke runs for mile after mile in an almost unbroken line, sometimes just a bank, but often aspiring to magnificent proportions.

The first objective on the crossing of the Clun hills is Panpunton Hill, a daunting prospect, especially if your day has only just begun and you are not properly into your stride. The path climbs 600 feet in a short half-mile. Between Knighton and the top of this hill there is no trace of the Dyke, and for the next two miles it is often no more than a hedgebank in size.

From Panpunton Hill you look south over Knighton and west along the Teme winding across its flood plain, dividing the hills of former Radnorshire from the hills of Salop. The wooded knoll of Castle Hill at the confluence of the Teme and Ffrwdwen Brook is the site of Cnwclas Castle where King Arthur is said to have defeated the giants. As far back as the fifteenth century there was a tradition that from a castle on the Green Mound (which is what Cnwclas means) Guinevere was married to Arthur. Her father was a local giant known as Gogyrfan (or Cogfan) Gawr. The castle was built by Roger Mortimer, it is thought, in about 1242, and remained for a long period in the hands of that family.

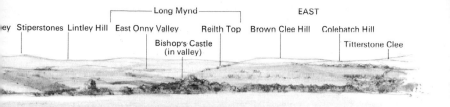

Long Mynd   EAST

ey Stiperstones Lintley Hill East Onny Valley   Reilth Top   Brown Clee Hill   Colebatch Hill

Bishop's Castle
(in valley)   Titterstone Clee

The view from Edenhope Hill

An easy route now runs north-westward from Panpunton Hill, either on or beside the Dyke, through a series of fields, to the Ordnance Survey column on Cwm-sanaham Hill, another fine viewpoint. The sharp angle of the Dyke here Fox believed to mark a fixed point where the earthwork was to pass over the highest part of the hill.

On the steep descent through gorse from Cwm-sanaham Hill towards Brynorgan the Dyke becomes intermittent. East ditch gives way to the normal west ditch. Considering the very dissected nature of the terrain the next portion of the Dyke retains a remarkably straight alignment. A road is crossed. Then over a rocky spur and over two streams the way continues to Garbett Hall Farm. It may be that during a spell of wet weather deep mire makes the path by the streams impassable. You might find it better to follow the road via Selley Hall Farm to Garbett Hall.

A clear, steadily rising track now begins the long ascent of Llanfair Hill, towards the highest point reached by the Dyke. The earthwork is of massive proportions and not until the path re-enters Powys does it dwindle significantly in scale. Llanfair Hill is a broad upland mass, dissected on both east and west sides by small stream valleys. In avoidance of these the Dyke for a while forgoes visual dominance of land to the west, keeping along the crest line of the hill. Untopped by fence or hedge, crossed by a minimum of field boundaries, it sweeps in a continuous ridge over the back of this hill. At 1,408 feet, where a green track is crossed, it is fitting that the Dyke should be at its finest and most inspiring.

For the half-mile before Springhill Farm no right of way was granted along the Dyke, so you must follow the quiet lane to the west. Where the Dyke Path turns right for a few yards at the cross-roads, in front of the farm, it is following an antiquity far older than the Dyke: the Clun–Clee Ridgeway. From Kerry Hill, along the ridge south of the Clun Valley, and north of Ludlow to Titterstone Clee and Bewdley   61

Teme Valley from Panpunton Hill. The wooded knoll of Cnwclas lies in the middle distance with the village below the viaduct

the route was followed by Neolithic axe-traders. In Clun numerous flint implements have been found (many are on show in the museum there), but the nearest flint is 80 miles away. This means that flint must have been imported into the area from outside, and conveyed westward. It came in, in fact, along two routes: via the Ridgeway itself along the watershed of the Clun and Teme; and also via what is now Stank Lane, south-east of Bishop's Castle, and along the watershed to Kerry Hill.

The Ridgeway later became a drove road from Newtown, for drovers and empty wagons from Wales avoiding the toll-gates in the Clun Valley. Nineteenth-century enclosure canalised the road. It became a rough track and later the metalled road it is now.

The Dyke Path descends 600 feet to the main Clun road at Lower Spoad Farm. Clun, the geographical and historical capital of the region, lies down-valley about three miles, and beyond it a whole

The Dyke at Hergan showing the right-angled turn. The Dyke, with a bank on the counterscarp, crosses the front of the view from left to right, before angling sharply north-west across *east-facing* slopes towards Edenhope Hill

group of villages taking their names from the river. If for nothing else these places will be remembered, it seems, for A. E. Housman's alliterative verse:

"Clunton and Clunbury,
Clungunford and Clun,
Are the quietest places
Under the sun."

Although Clun stands where two nominally main roads cross the river by a narrow medieval bridge, it still is a quiet town. The original motte and bailey castle, built by Roger Say, is one of the earliest castles along the Border. The present castle dates from the twelfth century. A winding street leads up to the Norman church with its massive tower. During the Civil War it was occupied by Parliamentary forces and partly burnt in a confrontation with the   63

Royalists. Sir Walter Scott at one time stayed at the "Buffalo Inn", where it is said he wrote *The Betrothed*.

Unless you are walking down to Clun then you cross the meadow opposite Lower Spoad, through the yard of Bryndrinog Farm, to the Newcastle–Whitcott Keysett road. Rare local buses run along this road to Clun.

On the steep ascent through the scrub beyond Bryndrinog Farm the course of the Dyke is very clear. Emerging on to open hillside, your way lies still uphill, soon on a Dyke lined with larch. Across the marshy head of a small stream the course of a more intermittent Dyke is followed through fields and woods and over streams towards the col at Hergan. As the Dyke bears north-eastward it becomes massive in scale with a high bank on the counterscarp. At the col a road and various trackways cut through the Dyke. None the less it is fairly easy to determine the remarkable right-angled alignment of the earthwork.

Fox considers the Hergan section, built by one gang and aligned along the *west* flank of the hill to its col, was almost certainly completed first. The second gang, working southwards towards the col, no doubt followed what was for them the most satisfactory alignment (the land is *east-facing*), but failed to meet the completed section of Dyke on the projected alignment, hence the awkward junction.

Beyond Hergan the path follows the Dyke through fields, via Middle Knuck Farm and up to the hilltop overlooking the Mainstone Valley. A swift descent between conifer plantations on a clear but often muddy track brings you to the isolated church of St John the Baptist, a mile away from Mainstone hamlet. This tiny church, considerably altered in the seventeenth and eighteenth centuries, is a pleasantly simple building. Inside, by the pulpit, is the boulder from which the hamlet is said to take its name. At one time, as a test of strength, it was the custom for village men to cast the boulder (weighing some two hundredweight) over their heads.

The long steep ascent on to Edenhope Hill is an effort well rewarded. For many this may rank as the best viewpoint on the whole walk. A descent into the Unk Valley brings you to the final climb on this crossing of the Clun district. When the open hilltop is reached the Dyke is on the grand scale, high-banked and narrow. A road crossing takes you into Powys again, and a pleasant farm track, in what was the ditch of the Dyke, brings another fine panorama.

The path drops steadily downward from the hills, across fields, to a lane at Cwm. An easy route continues northward, soon through the woods and plantations of Mellington Hall (caravan park and country club) to the main Montgomery road. A few yards farther and you cross the Caebitra, back into Salop and up to Brompton cross-roads and the old oak of the Blue Bell Hotel, symbolising good hospitality.

Ahead lies the prospect of easier walking, but duller. Apart from a brief excursion on to the Long Mountain it is maybe three or four days before you return to hill country, and many miles before the Dyke, now dwindled to a low bank, will be once more on the grand scale.

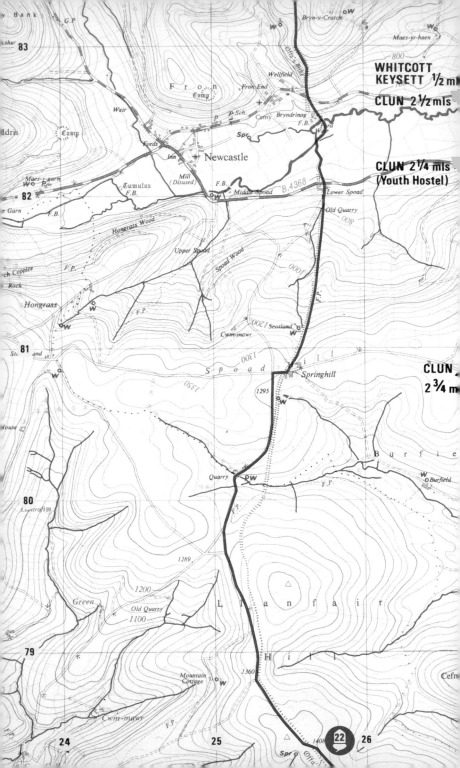

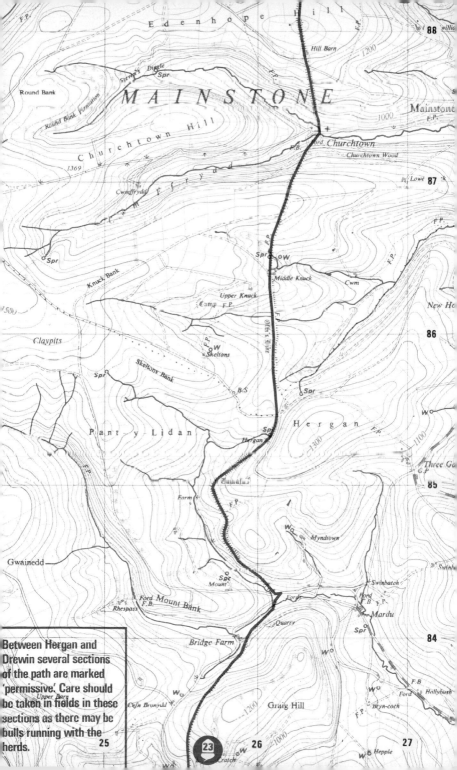

Between Hergan and Drewin several sections of the path are marked 'permissive'. Care should be taken in fields in these sections as there may be bulls running with the herds.

23

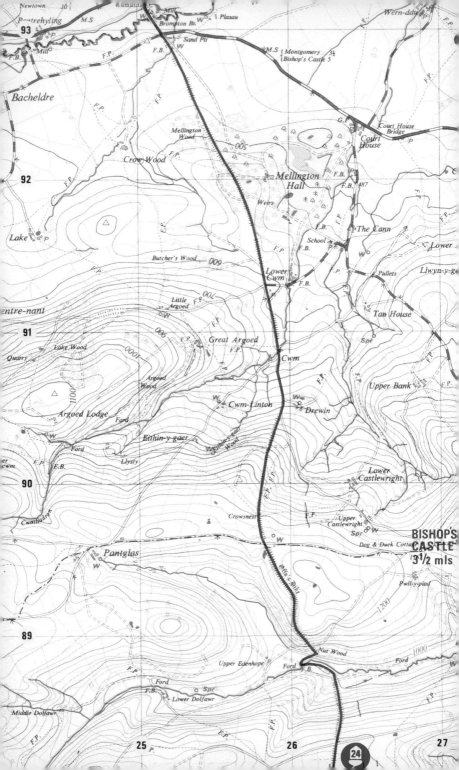

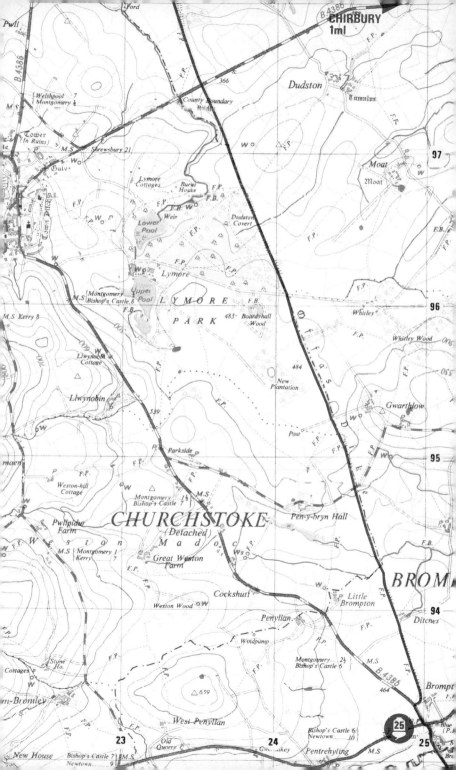

Brompton Hall to Llanymynech: the Severn corridor

And then they traversed the great plain of Argyngroeg as far as Rhyd-y-groes on the Severn. And a mile from the ford on either side the road, they could see the tents and the pavilions and the mustering of a great host.

The Dream of Rhonabwy (The Mabinogion)

Bounded on three sides by hills, the undulating Vale of Montgomery drains northward to the Severn. Across this landscape of broad, hedged fields and parkland the Dyke pursues a direct, if sinuous, course showing that originally this whole area must have been densely wooded. Though not large the Dyke is on the whole well defined and, considering this is now argicultural land, in a good state of preservation.

From Brompton Hall Farm, from field to field, now along the top of the Dyke, now beside it, the path, right on the boundary between Powys and Salop, runs an easy course: past Ditches Farm (so-called from the old name Offa's Ditch), over the Lack Brook, for a clear two miles to a driveway by the parkland of Lymore, a Jacobean black and white half-timbered house. By the time you reach the B4386 crossing, Montgomery Castle is dominating a wooded bluff to the west. Montgomery itself (Trefaldwyn) lies a mile from the path at the foot of the bluff.

Montgomery is an attractive town with several of the houses dating from Elizabethan and Georgian times. There is accommodation here, and a number of shops. If you are visiting the town the best point from which to begin an exploration is from the Iron Age camp above Ffriddfaldwyn. From the oldest settlement you can look north towards the Roman fort of Forden Gaer by the Severn, to Norman Old Montgomery at Hen Domen, and so make your way down via the "new" castle to New Montgomery, through something like 2,000 years of history.

The re-siting, during the 1220s, of the castle at a strategically safer site seems to have come about with the imminent threat of attack from the Welsh under Llywelyn the Great. During the wars against the two Llywelyns (the Great and ap Gruffydd) the town was sacked six times,

Montgomery

and later still by Owain Glyndŵr. After the Acts of Union Montgomery entered a more peaceful era. The poet George Herbert was born at the castle in 1593, and his elder brother, Lord Herbert of Chirbury, lived there during the Civil War. Some lines of another poet, John Donne, *The Primrose Being at Montgomery Castle upon the Hill, on which it is Situate,* symbolise the quieter times that prevailed:

> "Upon this Primrose hill,
> Where, if Heaven would distil
> A shower of rain, each several drop might go
> To his own primrose, and grow manna so;
> And where their form, and their infinity
> Make a terrestrial Galaxy,
> As the small stars do in the sky,
> I walk to find a true love...."

When Leland visited the town in the sixteenth century the need for fortification had obviously gone, for "great ruines of the waulle yet apere, and the remains of four gates, thus called, Kedewen Gate, Chirbury Gate, Arthur's Gate, and Kerry Gate". In the churchyard is the so-called Robber's Grave. In 1821 John Davies was hanged for robbery. Protesting his innocence he declared that no grass would grow on his grave if he had been unjustly hanged.

The Dyke Path continues to follow the Dyke, past Rownal Farm, on to the marshy levels of the Camlad. This has the distinction of being the only river flowing from England into Wales. Its course is an interesting one. In its upper course, in the vicinity of Bishop's Castle, it is flowing westward through a wide corridor across what was once 71 the floor of glacial Lake Camlad, whose waters were held back by ice in the Severn Valley. Where the Camlad now turns abruptly north through Marrington Dingle marks the point where escaping water from the lake excavated the four-mile-long gorge, after which it was able to flow due west towards the Severn.

While the Dyke heads straight across the river flats the footpath squelches leftwards to the road-crossing at Salt Bridge, and back to the Dyke at Pound House; then over Hem Hill, through the scattered houses at Forden and out to the road by Nantcribba Hall near the prominent tree-covered castle mound. The next half-mile is on the fast B4388, before you are once more following the Dyke through a succession of tiny hedged fields at Kingswood, to the metalled lane that follows the ancient Long Mountain ridgeway to Westbury. This lane is also on the line of an exceptionally straight section of Dyke, and of the Roman road from Viroconium (Wroxeter) to the important fort and settlement of Forden Gaer.

For all its extent, some eight miles from north-east to south-west, the sprawling mass of the Long Mountain reaches a mere 1,300 feet. On all sides it is dissected by steep dingles. Everywhere is covered with a deepish layer of stony clay known as head, and this has allowed the sheep and cattle pastures to continue right over the ridge, except on the west flanks which are covered by the extensive plantations of Leighton Park, under the protection of the Royal Forestry Society.

The Long Mountain and the Breiddens to the north, and the surrounding countryside, as an obvious zone from which to make incursions into Wales, were vulnerable to attack. Evidence of this exists in the various military and boundary works in the area: a hill fort, Roman road, Offa's Dyke, and several camps and castle mottes.

At 700 feet, a rising forestry track, on the line of a destroyed Dyke, leads from the road into the plantations of Green Wood. Soon the Dyke, damaged by repeated tree felling and erosion, is contouring the hillside at 800 feet, while the path is running parallel, but at a higher level. A wide view opens up across the estate of Leighton Park, across the Vale of Severn, and in the distance to Powys Castle. The hall, groves, church and series of contrived pools among the plantations of the Leighton estate are the brain-children of the nineteenth-century banker, Naylor.

The groves contain a remarkable variety of trees, including the Douglas Fir *(Pseudotsuga douglasii)*, the Giant Redwood *(Sequoia sempervirens)* and the Monkey Puzzle *(Araucaria araucana)*. As more varied and exotic plants were brought into this country during the eighteenth, but more particularly the nineteenth, century, so a fashion developed among the well-to-do for introducing these novelties into their gardens and estates. A specimen of Douglas Fir, the British Isles' tallest tree, grows to over 181 feet in the grounds of Powys Castle. The first reference to the Giant Redwood being grown in this country appeared in 1846. Then in 1856 the discovery that a plantation of Giant Redwood at Leighton was producing timber at a heavy rate resulted in its adoption for afforestation in milder districts in the south and west.

The footpath rejoins the Dyke briefly on a downward course through a Monkey Puzzle grove. The Dyke continues into a ravine, but the path begins its long but easy ascent to Beacon Ring: round the head of Offa's Pool to the Pentre road by open farmland; uphill through pastures; and finally to the great circular ramparts of the hill fort. The enormous rectangular construction seen on the side of the Long Mountain at Moel y Mab is the compost tank that provided fertiliser for the Leighton pastures.

The descent begins through Cwmdingle Plantation. Soon, as the path steepens through a series of fields, the Breiddens come into view over the shoulder of the hill. The chimneys you can see are at Buttington brickworks. A complicated route through small fields brings you to the old school house at Buttington on the B4388. In the field opposite, a low bank is identifiable as the Dyke. But it peters out before the Dyke Path reaches the Severn by Buttington Bridge, at a key point on this section of the long-distance path. Not until five miles away at New Cut does the Dyke re-appear.

The original ford here, the Rhyd-y-groes, was an easy route to Powys: a site of fierce battle and legend. Here in 894 the Saxons beat back invading Danes, only themselves to be beaten back a hundred years later by Gruffydd ap Llywelyn ap Seisyll. This, too, is the Rhyd-y-groes of Rhonabwy's dream in *The Mabinogion*, telling of "the mustering of a great host", of King Arthur, "seated on a flat island below the ford", and of the curious battle with the ravens of Owein.

Surrounded by road, railway and a scattering of buildings stretching along the road towards the purple shale quarries and the brick and tile works, it is hard to visualise great hosts encamped here, or engaged in pitched battle, or to imagine Henry Tudor's crossing of the ford in 1485 as, joining with the forces of Rhys ap Thomas, the future king rode on to Shrewsbury and to Bosworth.

Turning your back on the Shrewsbury road you cross over the river, where you can either continue along the Severn's west bank or catch a bus into Welshpool (Trallwng), two miles away. Unusual for Wales, this is a predominantly brick-built town, with many Georgian houses. The town gained borough status in 1282 in a rather unusual way. The princes of Powys, in hatred of their Welsh rivals, rather than through love of the English, more often than not ruled as self-styled barons. So it was that the Welsh prince Gruffydd ap Gwenwynwyn refused to submit a dispute to Welsh law when he created the borough, claiming he was a Marcher and therefore entitled to be judged as an English baron by common law.

The church in Welshpool dates from 542. It was rebuilt in 1275, and in 1866, with the typical insensitivity of the age to ancient church architecture, was rendered largely unrecognisable. At the end of the High Street is a house built in 1692 by Gilbert and Ann Jones who claimed that an ancestor, Richard, living in the reign of Edward VI, was the first Welsh Jones.

Undoubtedly one of the main reasons for detouring to Welshpool is to visit the seat of the princes of Powys, Powis Castle, set in extensive parkland to the south-west of the town. The impressive sixteenth-century castle, the Castell Coch (from its red sandstone walls), stands a quarter of a mile away from the original castle. When the Powys line failed the castle passed by marriage to the Cherletons (Charltons) of Shropshire who raised the oldest parts of the present Red Castle. 73

The Breidden

Captured in 1644 by the Parliamentarians, at the Restoration in 1722 it reverted to the Jacobite Earls of Powys (no connection with the princes of Powys). The castle is still a private residence, though in the care of the National Trust. In the eighteenth century, Lancelot ("Capability") Brown was engaged to design the gardens.

Perhaps for once car-borne "Dykers" have the advantage over walkers, since they can quickly move ahead to Llanymynech and avoid the less interesting interlude along the banks of the Severn, which is, if nothing else, straightforward. Through wide pastures the way is clear along the top of the flood embankment to the fast A483. Running parallel with the road, but on the other side of the fence, the path takes you to the towpath of the canal, still alongside the road. Beneath the grass in the nearby meadow beside the Severn are the faint traces of the Cistercian abbey of Ystrad Marchell (Strata Marcella), founded 800 years ago by Owain Cyfeiliog.

The next mile beside the canal to the lock and keepers' cottages at Pool Quay is pleasant. Pool Quay (Pool Stake, as it was known earlier) was the quay for "exporting", especially flannel goods from Welshpool to Shrewsbury on the Severn, and also to Liverpool. Once more across the A483 the Dyke Path follows the top of the flood embankment across wide pastures on these alluvial flats, beside an unattractive Severn meandering between steep muddy banks. Except where the fields are ungrazed the walking is easy. The redeeming feature is the

Chirk Castle seen across the Ceiriog Valley

Breiddens, a group of three steep-sided volcanic hills. The scene is marred, however, by quarrying on the face of the Breidden itself, and by the masts of the P.O. radio station.

On a clear day the view from the top of the hills extends as far as the Wrekin, the Arans, Plynlimon, and Cader Idris. The encampment of Cefn-y-castell on Middletown Hill is one of the many places where Caradoc is said to have fought his last battle. The Breidden was occupied during the Iron Age, and there are traces of an enormous camp there. The monument visible on the summit from the Dyke Path is the Rodney Pillar, erected in 1792 to commemorate the services of Admiral Sir George Rodney, and notably his victory at Dominica in 1782, a victory due more, perhaps, to the French admiral's lack of initiative. Rodney's second in command was "most exceedingly disappointed and mortified by the commander in chief... for not making a signal for a general chase the moment he hauled down that for the line of battle". Rodney has no connections with the Severn, the only possible link being that the woods in the area provided a considerable amount of oak for naval shipyards.

At length, down on the river plain, the embankment turns away from the Severn, over a flood gate, beside the New Cut to Derwas Bridge. A low bank in the adjoining field, hardly distinguishable from the many flood banks hereabouts, is the Dyke once more. Beyond the road at the Nea the Dyke is a low, spread bank, topped by massive 75 oaks, and running out to the B4393 west of the scattered hamlet of Llandrinio, whose weekly markets and two-yearly fairs once drew people all the way from Shrewsbury, sailing up the Severn, and on the Welsh side from Rhydescyn, Maesydd, Tir-y-mynach and many other places.

Over the B4393 the path leads via Hampton House Farm and the derelict station at Four Crosses, back yet again to the A483. With the limestone crags of Llanymynech Hill ahead to spur flagging spirits, you press on along the right-hand side of this fast and tedious main road, relentlessly following the line of the Dyke, to Llanymynech village. With luck, by the time you walk the Dyke Path the proposed rerouting along the towpath of the Shropshire Union Canal between Four Crosses and Llanymynech will have been approved and way-marked.

Early purple orchid

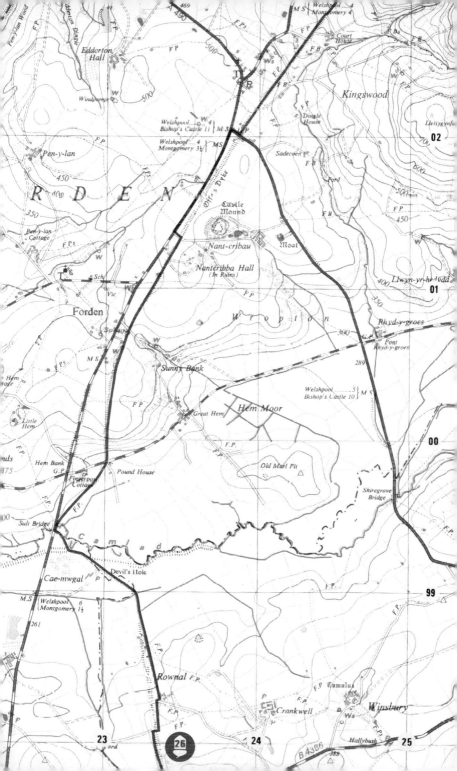

Stone House
Farm

cottage

gate
shed
gate

stiles

road

stiles

gate

farm

stile

WELSHPOOL
1 ml

27

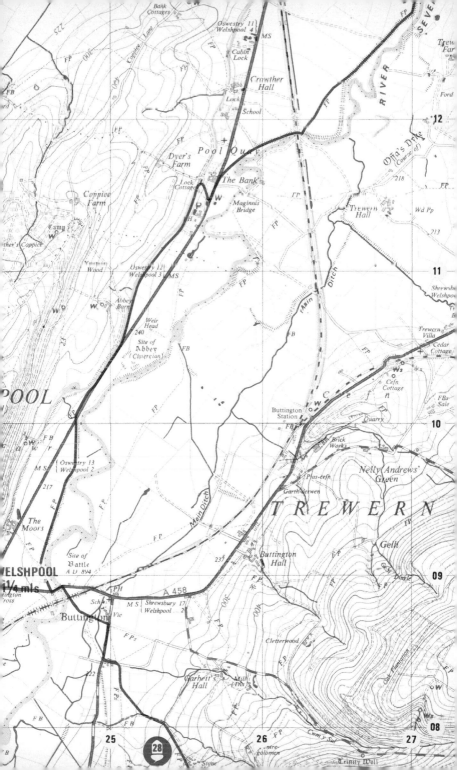

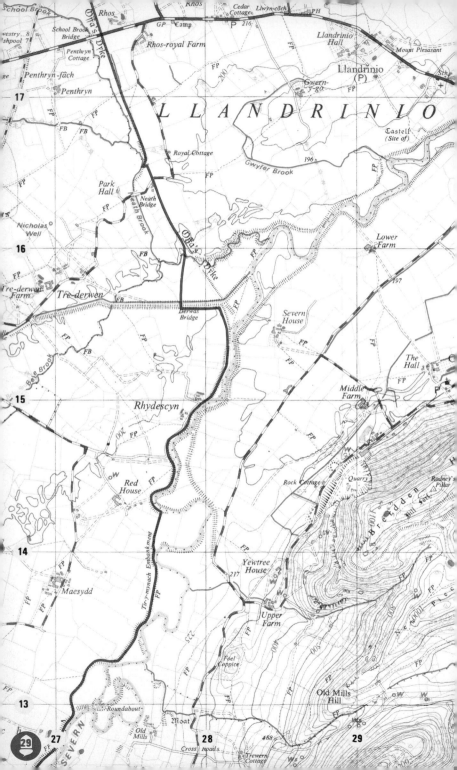

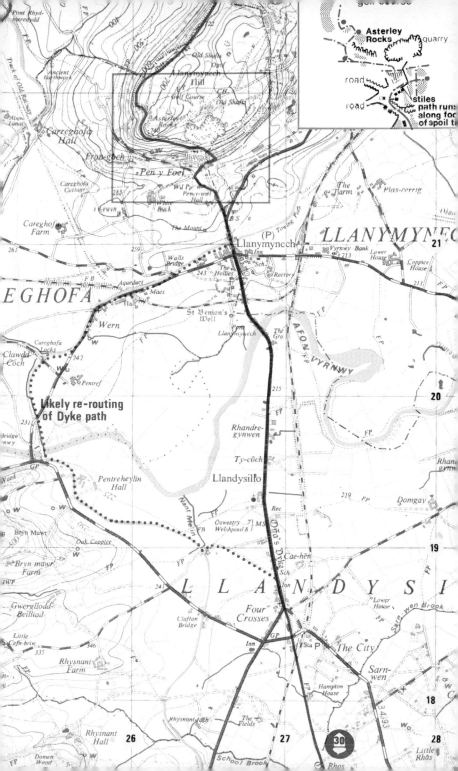

Llanymynech to Pentre: the eastern Berwyns

As Ozwestry, a pretie towne full fine,
Which may be lov'd, be likte and praysed both,
It stands so trim, and is maintayned so cleane,
And peopled is with folk that well doe meane;
That it deserves to be enrolled and shryned
In each good breast, and every manly mynde.

Thomas Churchyard

Despite its Welsh name Llanymynech is half in England, the line of the Dyke and national boundary passing through the houses on the right-hand side of the street. This rather uneventful cross-roads settlement, on rising ground above the Vyrnwy, is soon left behind where the main road heads into England. A quiet lane takes you over a rise to the cottages at Pen-y-foel, beneath the crags of Llanymynech Hill.

The limestone has been extensively quarried in the area, especially on Llanymynech Hill and in the hills north of Porth-y-waen. The long-distance path, searching out the optimum route through a complicated landscape of quarry, scattered settlement and farming, takes a switchback course avoiding the worst disfigurements.

As I said in the chapter on geology, mining and quarrying on Llanymynech Hill goes back to Roman times, when it is thought gold was among the minerals mined. Recent proof of gold in the area and the granting of permission to mine it suggests this may well have been so.

Rounding the foot of Asterley Rocks through a scattering of trees the path rejoins the Dyke running along the brow of the hill, where it coincides with the bank of a vast ancient hill fort. For a while your way lies beside a golf course beyond which are the vestiges of old workings. Steeply downhill, through woods the path (slippery when wet) leads to Porth-y-waen. The next mile or so is mainly on roads, to Nant-mawr. Beyond here a path through woods brings a welcome change of scene in the short turf of Moelydd. You may either cut straight across the side of the hill or make your way via the top at just 934 feet, marked by a rusty pole, placed here to mark the coming of age of a Trefonen landlord's son.

A track leading off the hill becomes a farm lane, beside low rocks, passing Ty-canol, to a road at Trefonen Hall. Midday may bring you to the "Efel Inn" at scattered Trefonen, and arrival at improved scenery.

Memories of a Dyke on the grand scale, steep-banked and undamaged, will be revived as you approach Pentre shannel. (Note the duck pond in the deepened ditch of the Dyke.)

The crossing of the lovely Morda Valley is marred only by the unsightly farm at Llanforda Mill. The climb from the valley is through beautiful beech and oak woods on the Llanforda estate, soon beside the Dyke, and past the whimsical stone bower set into its bank. At Racecourse Wood at the level of a rock crest the Dyke is cutting through the woods as a berm on the steep hillside, with a low bank on the west. The Dyke Path, however, keeps to higher ground through the wood, on its way to the open gorse heath on the Old Race Course above Oswestry. On a fine day this wide breezy ridge is a popular place for family outings, and you may feel slightly incongruous as you pick your way through aspiring footballers and past casual strollers to a road junction that looks one way to high rolling hills, and the other towards Oswestry and the Plain of Shropshire.

Perhaps not many walkers will wish to make the three-mile detour to Oswestry. But if you do you will find a pleasant enough place. The oldest settlement in the vicinity, Old Oswestry, is a massive Iron Age fort whose multiple ramparts enclose the summit of a drumlin. It lies on the line of the later Wat's Dyke. It was apparently held by the Romans and probably abandoned to the Saxons between 630 and 640. Old Oswestry's successor as the centre of a Saxon hundred was Maesbury, three miles to the south, which was in turn succeeded by the present Norman-founded Oswestry.

This was the base from which the Normans worked to gain the lands of northern Powys. Little now remains of the castle, squeezed between car park, market place and modern buildings.

Back on the Dyke Path no right of way was granted along the fine stretch of Dyke on Baker's Hill, and you are relegated to a mile of road. At Carreg-y-big, which takes its name from a megalith half a mile away to the north-west, your way is through fields and plantations by a magnificent Dyke to a small dingle by Orseddwon Farm. For a while the path lies east of the Dyke on a clear sandy track through the gorse and bracken of Selattyn Hill, some way from the tower on the hill top, set up last century to perpetuate the memory of a warrior, Gwen, killed here in a battle between the Saxons and Britons, a tale told in one of the poems of his father, Llywarch Hen.

Taking an easier route than the Dyke on the descent to the Morlas Brook, a track leads through scrub, past an old quarry, to a road junction. The second nineteenth-century stone marking the Dyke is uphill to the left. Over the Morlas Brook a farm track climbs steeply past a farm at Craignant. A short crossing of field paths brings you once more to the Dyke. The way is clear across roads and lanes, and the steep-sided wooded ravine of Nanteris, beside the last continuous stretch of Dyke you will meet. It is fitting it should be on the grand scale, if at times overgrown by invasive bracken. The climax comes as you top the hill above Nanteris and look across the deep Ceiriog Valley to massive Chirk Castle, rising from the woods on the opposite hill top.

On the north bank of the Ceiriog, reached after a steep descent across fields, is a small neat group of cottages which George Borrow visited last century with his guide, John Jones. " 'This bridge, sir', said John, 'is called the Pont-y-Velin Castell, the bridge of the Castle Mill; the inn was formerly the mill of the castle, and is still called Melin-y-Castell.' " The name Castle Mill survives; the inn does not.

You now have a choice of route. The main route, open all the year, leads via lanes to Crogen Wladys, and then through the outer parkland of Chirk Castle to Tyn-y-groes. The alternative route to Tyn-y-groes, beside the Dyke, takes you through the castle grounds and past the castle itself. This route is open only during the summer months when the castle is also open. This alternative, when open, is obviously preferable to the main route. For the first part of the climb, through woodland, the Dyke is absent altogether. This gap, known as the Adwy'r beddau, the gap of the graves, is traditionally the site of the ambush and defeat of Henry II by the Welsh at the Battle of Crogen in 1165.

At the castle, on fine days, a quieter battle is joined as, forsaking rucksack and boots, you mingle with the crowds who have come to Chirk the easy way. Chirk was one of the Border castles of Edward I in his conquest of Wales. Chirklands had been the property of Gruffydd ap Madoc, but in 1282, with Edward's victory over Llywelyn the Great, Gruffydd's son, Chirklands passed to Roger Mortimer. Six years later Edward was building at Chirk, either strengthening the original Castell-y-waun that stood there, or possibly starting work on the present castle. We know that the building of Chirk was largely the responsibility of Roger Mortimer, who completed the work in 1310.

The castle, now owned by the Myddleton family, has undergone considerable changes, largely in the eighteenth and nineteenth centuries, many of which were the work of Pugin. Only if you go down to the Chirk village entrance will you see the magnificent iron gates, constructed in the early eighteenth century by Robert and Thomas Davies.

From Tyn-y-groes where the alternative routes meet there is a mile and a half of road walking. Slowly the Dyke Path leaves the Berwyn foothills behind, trending down towards the Vale of Llangollen. The first view across the Vale as you are once again back on field paths near Plas-Offa (built on the Dyke) may come as a disappointment. In this area the path is approaching the edge of the Wrexham coalfield. Cefn Mawr with its chemical works (which you may nose out long before you see it) dominates the hill top a mile away.

This part of the Vale is best known, not for its scenic attractions, but for its industrial archaeology. In 1789 the Post Office made an attempt to extend the mail coach road service from Shrewsbury to Holyhead, but it was abortive. Within a week three horses had fallen. At the instigation of John Foster, Chancellor of the Irish Exchequer, Telford was engaged to examine and report on the route. Work on the proposed route took 15 years to complete, at an estimated cost, on the Chirk to Holyhead section alone, of £53,000 per annum over five years.

Between this road, now the A5, and the canal lies the last portion of Dyke on the long-distance path, large but overgrown. At Pentre, two fields away, you begin the final stages of the path, and possibly the finest walking of the whole journey.

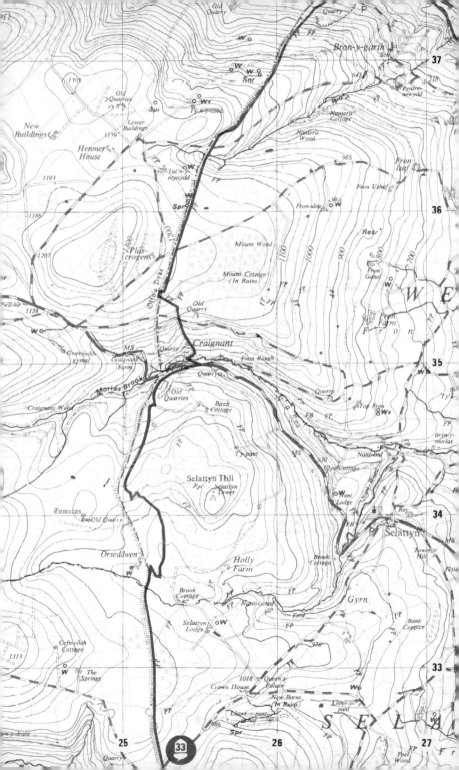

Concessionary route
via Pont-Cysyllte

Inset map labels:
roac
boatyard
Pont-Cysyllte
(aqueduct)
River Dee
canal
lifting
bridge
A5
B5434
Argced
Hall
A5

A539
railway
stile
stile
swing
gate
bridge under
railway
canal

Pentre to Llandegla:
the Vale of Llangollen

Thus consecrate to love in ages flown,
Long ages fled, Din's Branna's ruins shew,
Bleak as they stand upon their steepy cone,
The crown and contrast of the vale below,
Than screen'd by mural rocks with pride displays,
Beauty's romantic pomp in every sylvan maze.

Howel ap Einion Lygliw

When the Dyke is left behind, you step forward in time a thousand years into the era of canal building, which sets the theme for the next two miles.

In 1791 discussion began on a proposal to build a canal to serve agricultural Shropshire with coal and lime, and to tap the natural mineral resources of the Wrexham coalfield. When the chosen route received the Royal Assent on 30 April 1793, the problem of how the canal would be carried over the Dee and Ceiriog Valleys remained unresolved. This was the situation when Telford was appointed to the staff of the canal company in September of that year.

The foundation stone of his proposed high-level aqueduct was laid by Richard Myddleton of Chirk on 25 July 1795, but it was ten years before the bridge was completed. Even after its completion there was considerable doubt as to how the route north of the Dee would be carried out. Schemes for a tunnel through the hill at Cefn Mawr, for a long flight of locks, a vertical canal lift, and for an inclined plane were in turn abandoned. In the end a branch canal to Whitchurch was adopted as the main route by continuing it northward to join the Chester Canal at Nantwich.

And so it was that the canal over the aqueduct ended at Cefn Mawr. There was now no adequate water supply, so there was the additional expense of a navigable feeder along the Vale of Llangollen to Valle Crucis, where water could be drawn from the Dee. The opening ceremony was nevertheless a suitably grand affair. The surrounding hillsides were thronged with people as a procession of barges, one carrying a brass band, moved slowly over the aqueduct, to a fifteen-round cannon salute. It is a pleasant turn of fate that this, of all canals, should in recent years have come into its own as one of the most popular for pleasure boating.

90　　When the Dyke Path reaches the lifting bridge at Froncysyllte most

Plas Newydd with Castell Dinas Brân and the Eglwyseg Rocks as backdrop

walkers will continue on the concessionary footpath beside the canal as it turns away from the valley side on a great tree-grown embankment, to the high-level crossing of the Dee. As you step on to the aqueduct, already the valley is far below. The cast iron trough stretches 1,000 feet ahead, carried on stone piers 127 feet above the swirling waters of the Dee. George Borrow's guide described it as "the finest bridge in the world, and no wonder, if what the common people say be true, namely that every stone cost a golden sovereign. It gives me the pendro, sir, to look down".

If, like that guide, you suffer from vertigo, then the official route via the road bridge over the Dee does at least have the compensation of the best view of the aqueduct itself. The alternatives meet near Trevor, where you begin to head for wilder scenery. Beyond the A539 you are soon climbing steadily through plantations above decaying Trevor Hall. At length you emerge above the trees on to a quiet road, among heather and gorse and rocky slopes, high above the Vale of Llangollen. Though the next three miles are on road, unless you are here on a fine weekend in high summer this road, known locally as the Precipice Walk, is deserted. It begins to descend, unfenced, across rocky hillside, beneath the towering limestone crags of Trevor and Eglwyseg Rocks.

For five miles the great buttresses of these rocks run along the north side of the Vale and into the Eglwyseg Glen, and for almost their entire length the Dyke Path keeps with them.

Castell Dinas Brân, on its steep shaly knoll, becomes dominant in the scene. Paths lead to its summit, and it would be a fitting end to a day's walking to descend from here into Llangollen, which could serve as a base for a day or two from which to explore the surrounding places of interest before you move north again.

The castle was built by the thirteenth-century prince of Powys, Gruffydd ap Madoc, son of the founder of Valle Crucis Abbey, on the site of an Iron Age fort. It is not surprising therefore that Llangollen, which developed where the markets were originally held, should seem more akin to the lands of Powys in former Montgomeryshire than to

91

Clwyd. Dinas Brân, Borrow tells us, was once quite impregnable, serving as a retreat to Gruffydd from his countrymen when he sided with Edward I. "But though it could shield him from his foes it could not preserve him from remorse and the stings of conscience, of which he speedily died." Today only crumbling walls remain:

> "Gone, gone are thy gates, Dinas Brân on the height!
> The warders are blood-crows and ravens, I trow;
> Now no one will wend from the field of the fight
> To the fortress on high, save the raven and crow."

Llangollen, a mile away, is entered across the fourteenth-century Dee bridge (widened), still known as one of the seven wonders of Wales. If the nineteenth-century architecture is prosaic and functional, it certainly is not the "dirty, ill-built and disagreeable town" the Reverend W. Bingley described. Llangollen was discovered during the coaching era when it was a popular posting station on the Holyhead road. Nowadays in summer it is a popular tourist centre, famous principally for the July Eisteddfod, held here every year since 1947. It takes its name from the church of St Collen, a double-aisled building whose superb timber roof, carved with angels, flowers and animals, is thought to have been brought from Valle Crucis.

A little above the town is Plas Newydd, the black and white timbered home of Eleanor Butler and Sarah Ponsonby, the Ladies of Llangollen, two famous recluses from the Irish aristocracy who settled here in 1791. It was a plain stone-built house when they moved in, but a custom developed for guests to bring carved panels of wood as presents, so that by the time they died, Eleanor Butler in 1829 and Sarah Ponsonby in 1831, the house had become embellished throughout. Sir Watkin Williams Wynn of Wynnstay, the greatest landowner in the area, Lord Myddleton of Chirk, Edmund Burke, and Scott, Wordsworth and Shelley were among the famous visitors to Plas Newydd.

If you follow the canal out of Llangollen and then north towards the Horseshoe Pass on the main road, you will come to Valle Crucis where "the fine gothic west end embowered in trees, and backed by the mountain on whose summit stand the shattered remains of Castell Dinas Brân, form a scene finely picturesque".

Valle Crucis Abbey, a colony of Strata Marcella whose faint traces were passed at Pool Quay, was founded in 1201 by Madoc ap Gruffydd. The church and some of the monastic buildings date from the first quarter of the thirteenth century. But fire destroyed much of the site, and extensive alterations were subsequently made. Following the suppression by Henry VIII the site passed to Sir William Pickering. After many changes of ownership the abbey passed in 1950 into the custodianship of the Ministry of Works, now absorbed into the Department of the Environment.

The abbey and its glen take their names from the ancient Pillar of Eliseg, the remains of a high cross, standing in a field a quarter of a mile up-valley from the abbey. The cross was thrown down in the Civil War and only the upper part remains. An inscription on the pillar, set up in honour of Eliseg, partly contemporary with Offa, tells of his

uniting the inheritance of Powys (laid waste for nine years) after

Pillar of Eliseg

wresting it from the hands of the English, with fire and the sword. This is probably a reference to the withdrawal of the Saxons from the line of their original incursions, marked by the short dykes, to the agreed Offan frontier.

The Pillar stands on an artificial mound found to contain a tomb, with a body set about with blue stones. The tomb is thought to date from the fifth, or early sixth, century, and evidence, slim as it is, suggests the body may be that of Cadell Ddyrnllug, ancestor of Eliseg.

From Llangollen you may rejoin the Dyke Path via Dinas Brân or follow the lane past Dinbren Isaf which supplied the Ladies of Llangollen with butter and turkeys. Soon the road is left behind, and a path takes you across the stony bed of a stream to contour the scree below the crags. In summer rampant bracken makes the going rough. Gradually the path climbs up through the scree, the scenery becoming wilder and more rugged. The official route contours the hillside below Craig Arthur, but it is also possible to follow the path up through the rocks on to the extensive undulating plateau top of Eglwyseg Mountain, as shown on map No. 37 (page 96). Only a short distance beyond the routes join again, to descend through larches and a plantation to rejoin the road at the remote ford of World's End, aptly named unless you happen to arrive on a fine weekend when the litter of cars makes this place anything but remote.

Following the road uphill towards Minera you will see signs of nineteenth-century lead mining. Beyond the plantations, trees give way altogether to sombre heather moorland. An Offa's Dyke Path   93 plaque marks the place to leave the road at the highest point on its crossing to Minera. A line of posts indicates the way through rampant heather and marshy hollows on this crossing of featureless Cyrn y Brain. The moor is far more extensive than might appear from the map, and the worst is not over when the fence is reached across the centre of the plateau. The whole of the north side of the grouse moor has been deep-ploughed, and planted with conifer seedlings. You tumble across the deep furrows towards (hopefully) Hafod Lon (originally Hafod Bilston). Until waymarking is complete in this section, a compass bearing of 295° from the stile in the moorland fence should bring you to a small weir at the head of a ravine above the farm. Navigation once more becomes straightforward.

The route lies along roads to Llandegla, a small stone village strung out along a single street, on rising ground above the Alyn. At 850 feet this is the highest settlement along the Dyke Path. At an obvious stage too on the footpath you may wish to find accommodation in the hamlet or nearby.

Black grouse (male)

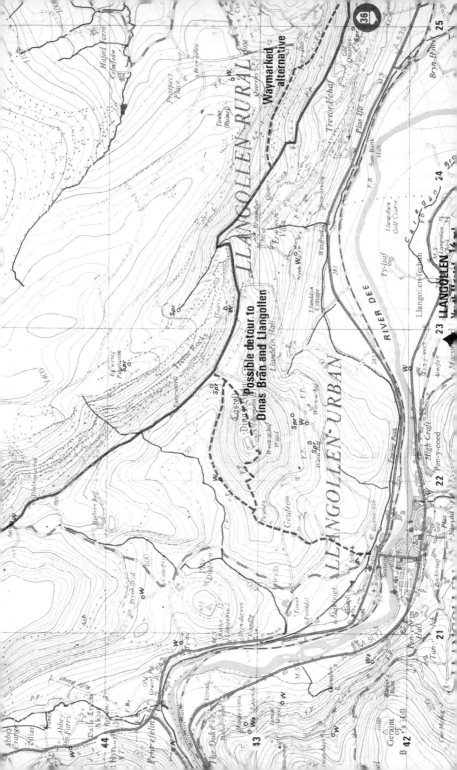

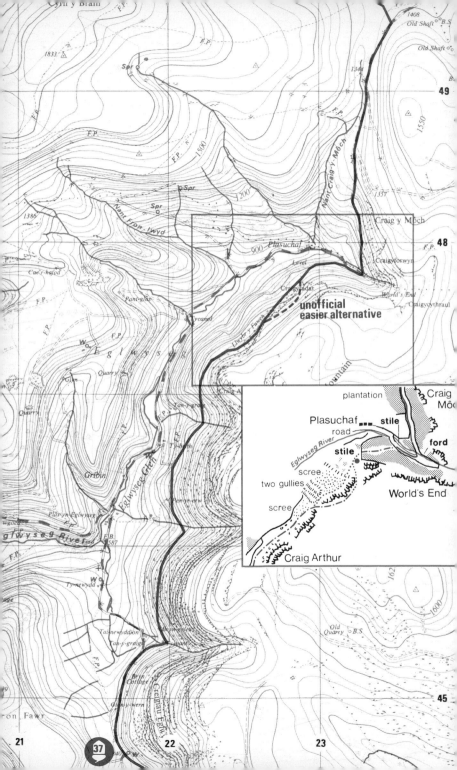

unofficial
easier alternative

plantation

Plasuchaf

stile

road

Eglwyseg River

stile

scree

two gullies

scree

Craig
Môch

ford

World's End

Craig Arthur

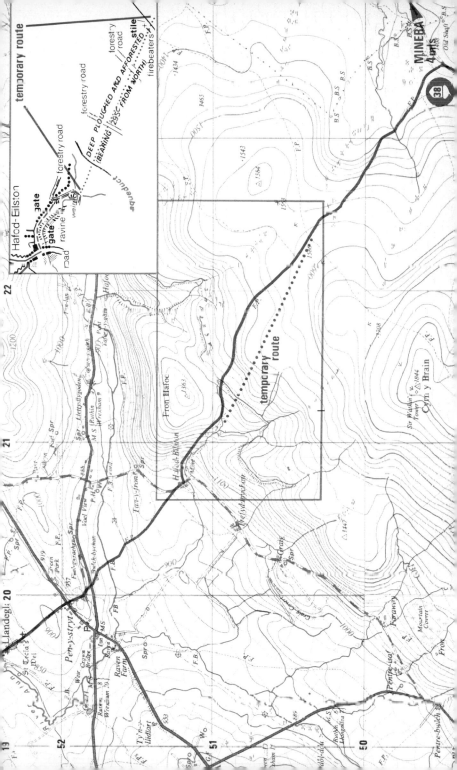

temporary route

forestry road

forestry road

DEEP PLOUGHED AND AFFORESTED
(BEARING 255° FROM NORTH)

forestry road

aqueduct

Hafod-Elston

gate

gate

ravine

road

forestry road ——————
forestry road · · · · · · · ·
stile +
firebeaters +

Fron Hafoc

Hafod-Bwaidd

temporary route

MINERA

38

Llandegla to Bodfari:
the southern Clwydians

*About three miles to the north is a range of lofty
mountains, dividing the shire of Denbigh from that of
Flint, amongst which . . . , and lifting its head high above
the rest, is the mighty Moel Vamagh, the mother heap.*

George Borrow: *Wild Wales*

Stretching for over 20 miles the long, narrow line of the Clwydian
Range marks the boundary between the more industrial landscape
around Deeside and the remoter countryside of former Denbighshire.
On the east and less spectacular side, the Clwydians present an
irregular flank of hills. On the west a near-continuous scarp slope
rises sharply above the Vale of Clwyd, that "most pleasant, fruitful,
populous and delicious vale, full of villages and towns", as Defoe called
it. It is a pity that some of the openness of these hills is being lost to
forestry interests which have planted large areas near Moel Famau
and Penycloddiau.

The hard 18 miles from Llandegla to Bodfari are too much in one
day for any but strong walkers. Fortunately there are several places
where you will be able to break your journey and descend east or west
from the hills, to either a small village or, a short bus ride away, one of
the towns in the area.

A series of damp pastures, crossed by the Alyn, characterises the
first mile of footpath beyond Llandegla, to the B5431, beyond the low
limestone outcrops near which a complex group of prehistoric burial
mounds was excavated a century ago. The path begins to rise steadily
via Chweleiriog and Tyddyntlodion Farms to Moel y Waun which,
with Moel yr Acre, forms the southernmost hill of the Clwydians. As
you proceed from one height to the next Ruthin is at first dominant in
the Vale below, but later it is Denbigh, and finally St Asaph.

The path climbs steadily over little Moel y Gelli, beside a
plantation, and then more steeply on to the heather of Moel y Plas,
above Llyn Gweryd, with a fine view back over the Alyn Gap. At the
col between Moel y Plas and Moel Llanfair a lane runs down to the
limestone country around Llanarmon-yn-iâl, a pleasant stone-built
hamlet beside the Alyn. *Iâl* was adopted as a surname by a local

family, one of whom, Elihu Yale, founded Yale University.

The Dyke Path contours the slopes of Moel Llanfair, and bears round the col leading to Moel Gyw, past the Garreg Lŵyd boulder marking an ancient path over to Llanarmon. Gradually you drop down to one of the main passes through the hills where the main road from Mold winds its way over to Ruthin. Here you may take a bus down into the Vale for a night's lodging and explore this ancient town, perched on its ridge of sandstone.

The heart of Ruthin is the market place, St Peter's Square. On its south side the bank occupies what was once the courthouse and prison. An arm of the original gallows can still be seen as a beam above the right of the westernmost dormer window. In Castle Street, off the square, and in its neighbouring streets, are some of Ruthin's oldest buildings. In Well Street is the site of the Wynnstay Arms Hotel, formerly the "Cross Foxes", where George Borrow dined with his guide. The only house not destroyed during Glyndŵr's raid in 1400 is at No. 2. The sandstone castle (not open to the public) was founded by Edward I in 1281 on the site of an earlier stronghold, and granted to Reginald de Grey.

The church, towards the north end of the ridge, dates from 1310 when there were two churches side by side, one for the parishioners, the other for the monastic priests. After the Reformation the collegiate church went into disuse, and was finally demolished. The present church contains a fine carved roof, presented by Henry VII.

The path leaves the A494 beyond the Clwyd Gate. The official route climbed over Gyrn and Moel Eithinen, but conflicting interests have disputed the right of way. An alternative but less interesting route follows the track to the east, above Moel-eithinen Farm, to the col below Foel Fenlli.

A steep climb, angling up through the heather, brings you over the huge ramparts of the Iron Age hill fort that crowns the summit, the first of the chain of forts along the Clwydians. Its banks reach as much as 25 feet above the outer ditch on the north and east sides. Moel Famau's strange Jubilee Tower is clearly in view as you descend sharply to the narrow road and the crowds at Bwlch Pen-Barras, following an old routeway used by the Beaker folk between Foel Fenlli and the hills above Nannerch.

Fortunately most of the visitors to the Bwlch seem more attached to their cars than their surroundings and you are soon following a clear

The view from Moel Llys-y-coed

Vale of Clwyd | Irish Sea | Penycloddiau | Moel y Parc | Moel Arthur | NORTH | Moel Plas-yw track, in places almost a highway, across open land, to the windswept summit of the Clwydians at just 1,820 feet, and their finest viewpoint. Forty miles away you will see Snowdon and Cader Idris on a clear day, and Runcorn and Crosby in the other direction. The sea is unmistakable.

Moel Famau, far more so than its neighbours, seems to catch the full force of the wind. On one occasion in 1862 the wind was so strong as to cause the Jubilee Tower to collapse. The present squat structure is all that remains of the original two-tiered obelisk set up in 1810 to mark the jubilee of George III.

The Dyke Path continues on a fine ridge walk over Moel Dywyll, rounding the slopes of Moel Llys-y-coed, to face the bastion of Moel Arthur, its bald summit crowned by a near-circular fort. From the road over the col below Moel Llys-y-coed you scramble up the precipitous side of Moel Arthur whose 340 acres of rough moorland have been approved as a country park. From the last major viewpoint on the footpath you follow an easy path down to the quiet road leading to Nannerch. The half-mile climb to the vast summit fort of Penycloddiau is through the edge of a plantation. Arrival at the ramparts of the hill fort brings a return to better walking as you follow the massive earthwork for almost half a mile to the huge double ramparts on its north side.

The path declines the next inviting hill of Moel y Parc, un-named on O.S. maps, but distinguishable by the B.B.C. TV mast on its slopes, preferring to follow lanes and pleasant grassy tracks gradually downhill to the farms and cottages near Waen. The crossing of the Wheeler marks the end of a superb section of Dyke Path. You will find accommodation in Bodfari; or, if you prefer, you can take a bus into Denbigh and explore the second of Edward I's garrison towns in the Vale of Clwyd. In contrast to Ruthin, with its red sandstone castle, Denbigh is dominated by a limestone castle on a bluff above the Afon Ystrad.

But like Ruthin, Denbigh came into Edward's possession after the capture of David, brother of Llywelyn, prince of Wales. When Llywelyn in his campaign against Edward had been slain at Builth, David assumed sovereignty, and summoned his chieftains to the small hill fortress at Denbigh, where it was resolved to continue the war. After his victory over David, Edward granted Denbigh to Henry de Lacy, Earl of Lincoln, who built the town walls and began the castle in 1282. The castle was reduced to a ruin by Charles II.

"Through every arch or hole in the wall some gentleman's house or some elegant ornamental building or some solemn wood or some cultivated hill whose gentle rise seems contrived on purpose to shew the enclosures on its side, are discovered, and each view is called the most beautiful till another is examined." So Mrs Thrale described the view when she came to Denbigh Castle with Dr Johnson in 1774. Johnson himself, apparently unaware of the view, dismisses the castle as "a prodigious pile . . . now so ruined that the form of the inhabited part cannot easily be traced".

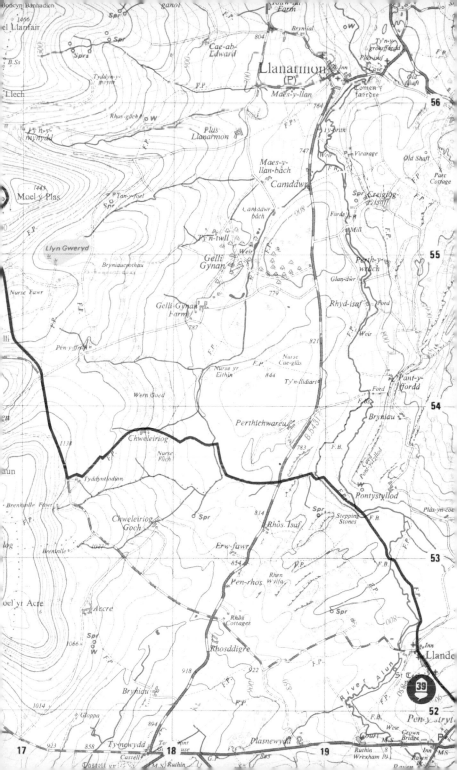

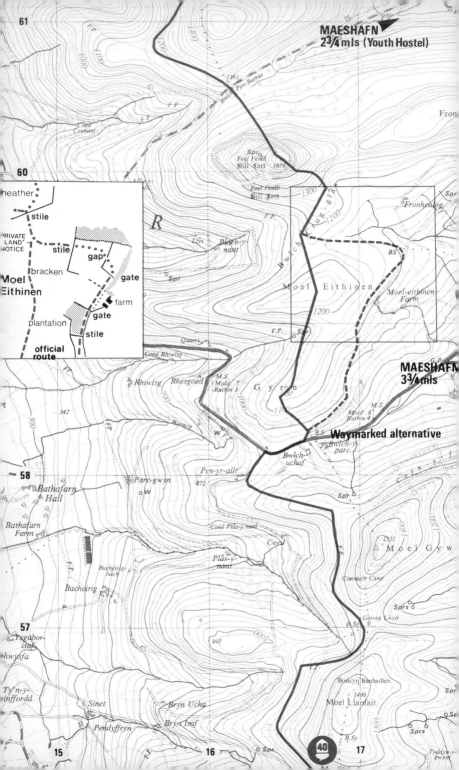

MAESHAFN
2¾ mls (Youth Hostel)

MAESHAFN
3¾ mls

Waymarked alternative

Inset map

PRIVATE
LAND
NOTICE

heather

stile

stile

gap

bracken

gate

Moel
Eithinen

farm

gate

plantation

stile

official
route

40

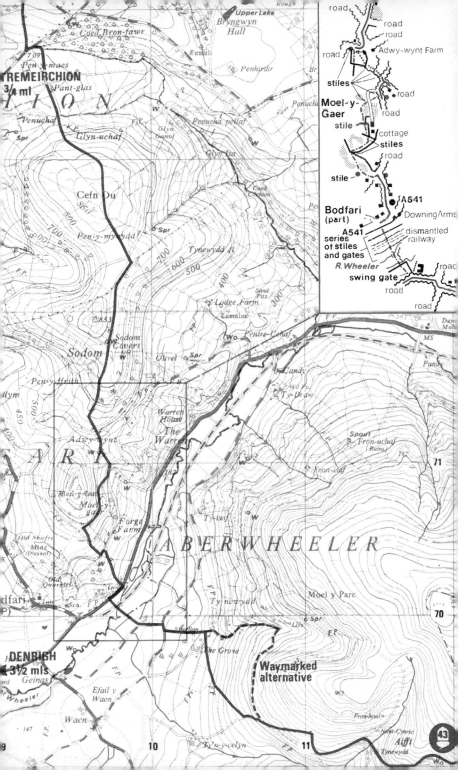

Bodfari to Prestatyn:
the northern Clwydians

Lovely the woods, waters, meadows, combes, vales,
All the air things wear that build this world of Wales.

Gerard Manley Hopkins: *In the Valley of the Elwy*

At the Wheeler Gap the high open hills of the Clwydians are left behind. Across the northern Clwydians the footpath wanders back and forth as if reluctant to meet the sea. A good deal of road walking in some sections, and an intricate route through small fields in others are offset by surprisingly wide panoramas along the Welsh coast, from the Great Orme at Llandudno, past the sprawl that is Rhyl at the mouth of the Clwyd, to the landscape of power on Deeside. Along the footpath, bracken slopes and mixed woodland coverts, plantations and small villages are set among a pattern of hedged fields.

The final stage of the footpath begins on the outskirts of Bodfari village. The centre of the village, on rising ground, lies grouped round the church a quarter of a mile off the main Denbigh–Mold road. At Ffynnon Ddeier, a well a few hundred yards from the church, it was once the custom to immerse children up to their necks to prevent their crying at night.

Over the flank of Moel-y-Gaer, topped by its small hill fort, the path crosses pasture land to the lane at Sodom, notable only for its name. In Cefn Du there is a brief return to more open land. The corner of Prestatyn now appears round the scarp of the hills. There follows a mile of road walking on the lanes above Tremeirchion, a small village on a narrow outcrop of limestone. A quarter of a mile north of the village caves excavated in the limestone in 1886 revealed the remains of prehistoric animals, one of the most significant prehistoric finds in the area.

The footpath goes over the side of Moel Maenefa to another lane, but turns off across fields before you reach St Beuno's College, where Gerard Manley Hopkins, training to be a priest, lived for several years, inspired by the Clwydians, the Vale and the Valley of the Elwy to his most ecstatic poetry.

The footpath drops down to the A55 at the hamlet of Rhuallt, thought to lie on the line of the Roman road from Deva via the posting station of Varae, which some believe to be present-day St Asaph, to the fort at Canovium in the Conway Valley and eventually to Segontium (Caernarvon). No trace of the road remains, and its precise course is under some dispute among historians.

St Asaph, the smallest of cities, is just three miles away on a slight rise between the Clwyd and the Elwy, from which it derives its Welsh name of Llanelwy. The cathedral, appropriate to the size of the village-city, is the smallest in England and Wales, just 182 feet long. Its origins date back to a monastery and church founded as early as 550 by St Cyndeyrn (St Kentigern of Cumberland), first bishop of Glasgow, when he sought refuge in Wales after being driven from his see by persecution. On his return north he nominated the scholar Asa (Asaph) as his successor. No trace remains of the earliest building, constructed of wood. The oldest remaining parts, a doorway and parts of the chancel, belong to the Norman church, burnt to the ground by the forces of Edward I. The rebuilt cathedral was again burnt, by Owain Glyndwr in 1402, and once more repaired. Sir Gilbert Scott was responsible for the nineteeth-century restoration.

Beyond Rhuallt you climb up the scarp through woodland, and across the side of Mynydd y Cwm. Rights of way across the hill top are restricted by the plantations of Ffrith Fawr, which means you once more must tread hard roads. The footpath is gradually drawing near to the line of Offa's Dyke, just two and a half miles away to the east beyond the eighteenth-century artificial Lake Helyg in its setting of trees.

On Moel Hiraddug, which you skirt on its east by Tyddyn-y-cyll, is the last of the Clwydian hill forts, where excavations are being carried out before quarrying destroys it. On its north side the older part of the village of Dyserth commands a wide view. The village is best known for the stream, fed from the Ffynnon Asaph a mile away, that falls 40 feet down a limestone rock, and flows through the centre of the village.

Field paths and green trackways take the Dyke Path past St Asaph's Well, whose strong spring (supplying four million to five million gallons of water a day) Prestatyn U.D.C. has despoiled. In adjoining Marian Mill the old water wheel can still be seen behind the Offa's Dyke Path signpost. The path continues through the dell near Henfryn Hall and over farm land west of Gop Hill, conspicuous a short mile away by its summit burial mound, one of the largest in the country. On its slopes the last traces of the Dyke have been found. A mile away to the west Dyserth Castle once stood on a summit of limestone. Its time of foundation is unknown, though it was fortified by Henry III in about 1241, and later destroyed by Llywelyn ap Gruffydd.

A greater castle than Dyserth still stands not far away on a low hill above the Clwyd overlooking Morfa Rhuddlan (Rhuddlan Marsh), "wild in its situation, rude in its appearance, the haunt of screaming gulls and clamourous rooks". Rhuddlan, at the lowest crossing point on the Clwyd, was a key point in Border warfare until the end of the twelfth century. The castle, founded early in the tenth century, was the seat of Gruffydd ap Llywelyn when it was taken by Harold in 1063. Although rebuilt by the Welsh, it later came under Robert of 107

Rhuddlan who began to strengthen the site. For over 200 years possession of the castle swayed back and forth between the Welsh and English. In 1188 Archbishop Baldwin and Giraldus Cambrensis were entertained there by Dafydd, son of Owain Gwynedd.

The castle was finally captured by Edward I in 1277 and rebuilt a year later in its present rectangular form above the Clwyd. It was from Rhuddlan Castle that Edward duped the Welsh into accepting his infant as Prince of Wales, as one whose life was irreproachable, and who had never spoken a word of English.

Continuing on its way the footpath runs on to the open common land at Tan-yr-allt, skirting above the old quarry face, and on to the scarp overlooking the sprawl of Prestatyn. In contrast, to the south and east, is the hamlet of Gwaenysgor and its surrounding farm land. Gwaenysgor is barely a mile from the outskirts of Prestatyn but at 600 feet above it, separated by the steep scarp, it is strangely remote. Its church is pleasantly simple. The location of the Drws y Cythraul (The Devil's Door) can still be seen on its north side. This was used only to admit into the church the unbaptised or the excommunicated who had repented and done penance. Once the person had entered the church the door would be slammed to keep the Devil out.

As you follow the path over Coed yr Esgob, through the gorse and scrub, you still feel curiously detached from Prestatyn. That feeling is soon dispelled as you descend the scarp to join the line of the Dyke for its last mile to the sea through the respectable suburbs. Prestatyn has few historical associations apart from the Dyke, although it once possessed a castle built probably by Llywelyn, prince of Wales. Only a few foundations now remain, east of the town. Until the coming of the railway in 1848 Prestatyn was no more than a cluster of fishermen's houses with an inn, "The Cross Foxes", passed at the bottom of the Fforddlas.

You will feel quite out of place as you make your way down High Street and along Bastion Road to the sea front, amid the holiday-makers and trippers, the gift shops, the ice cream and the candy floss. But as you reach the sea it will be with satisfaction and a sense of achievement. You can let your mind's eye wander southwards from this sea, along the whole line of Clwydian hills, through the Vale of Llangollen, along the Dyke, through the many and varied miles of the Border to that other sea at the grey boulder on Sedbury Cliff. If you have gone at a leisurely pace, and taken time to explore, your experience of the Border will be of a landscape of infinite variety and complexity, rich in historic associations. If Chepstow's sprawling suburbs, parts of the Monmouthshire lowlands, and the Severn Valley were necessary to achieve this, they will have been worth it.

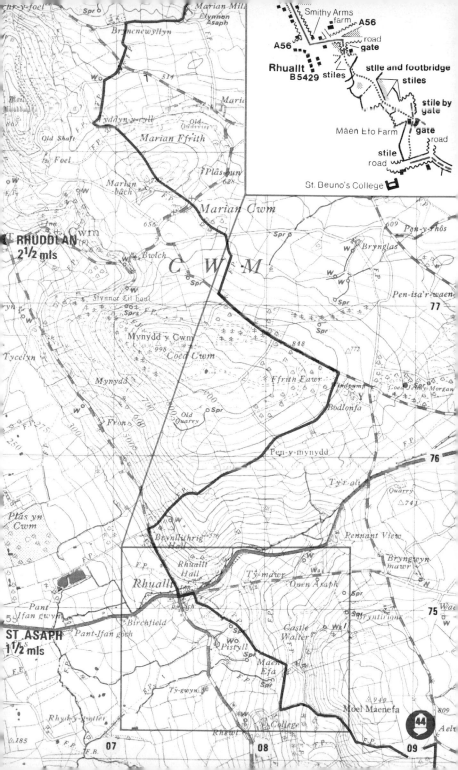

Smithy Arms
farm **A56**
road
gate
Rhuallt
B 5429 stiles stile and footbridge
stiles

stile by
gate

Màen Efo Farm gate
road

stile
road

St. Beuno's College

Marian Mill
Elynnen
Asaph
Bryncnewyllyn

Spr
Wo
514

Tyddyn-y-ryll
Marian Ffrith
Old Quarry
Marian
bâch
Plâs-bun
628

Marian Cwm

RHUDDLAN
2½ mls
Cwm
Bwlch
C · W · M
Bryncglas
Pen-y-rhôs
Spr
Wo

Pen-isa'r-waen
77

Mynydd y Cwm
Coed Cwm
998
Ffrith Fawr
Bodlonfa
Coed Jolly-Morgan
772

Tycelyn
Mynydd
Fron
Old Quarry
Spr
Pen-y-mynydd
Ty-r-ali
Quarry
741
76

Plâs yn
Cwm
Brynllithrig
Hall
Rhuallt
Hall
Ty-mawr
Owen Asaph
Rennant View
Bryngwyn
mawr

ST. ASAPH
1½ mls
Rhuallt
Pant
Ifan gwyn
Birchfield
Pant-Ifan goch
Castle
Walter
Bryntirion
75

Pistyll
Spr
Màen
Efa
Ty-gwyn
Moel Maenefa

Rhyd-y-trofer
College
Rhewl
44
Aelw
809

07
08
09

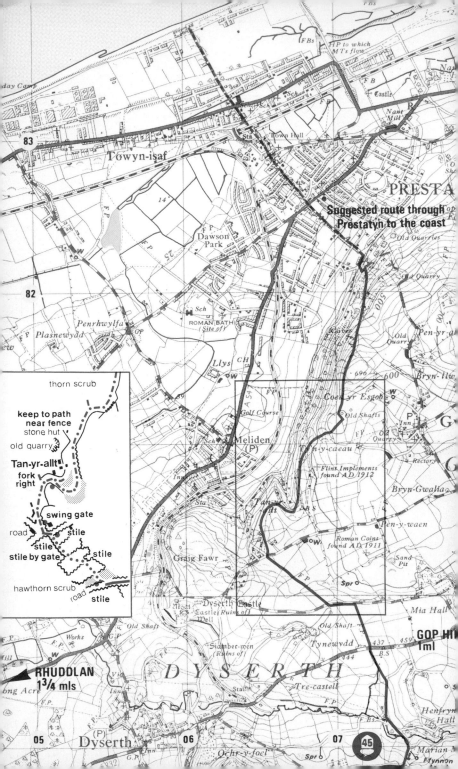

Suggested route through Prestatyn to the coast

thorn scrub

keep to path near fence
stone hut
old quarry
Tan-yr-allt
fork right
swing gate
road · stile
stile
stile by gate · **stile**
hawthorn scrub
road · **stile**

Facilities for walkers

Some advice

A complete coast to coast walk could be made in a fortnight, averaging about 12 miles a day. This will leave little time to stop off on the way, and you will be left with only a fleeting impression of places passed. With three weeks there is more time to explore and gain a richer impression of the Border.

When you set out along the Dyke Path:

ALWAYS CARRY ESSENTIAL EQUIPMENT FOR AN EMERGENCY. This includes a wrist watch, compass (and know how to use it), Ordnance Survey maps of the area, at least 1:63,360 scale, a torch with spare battery in case you are caught out in the hills at night, a whistle, a First Aid kit, and energy-giving food (Kendal mint cake, glucose tablets, sultanas, chocolate, for example).

WEAR THE PROPER CLOTHING, AND BE PREPARED FOR ANY WEATHER. Remember, weather changes in the hills are far more rapid than on lower ground: mist and rain can descend in a matter of seconds. It would be unwise to attempt the walk without proper footwear, which includes strong hiking boots and fell boots, though these latter are scarcely waterproof. Wellington boots give quite inadequate support and little grip on clayey slopes. Woollen rather than nylon socks or stockings should be worn, two pairs for extra comfort. An anorak or similar waterproof jacket with a hood is ideal, and should come below the waist to keep wind and rain off the small of the back. Carry at least one spare pullover. What you wear below the waist is a matter of personal taste, provided it is reasonably warm. You may find waterproof overtrousers a useful extra, especially where the path is through bracken or long grass wet with rain or dew, but don't expect miracles of them. Likewise a cagoule is useful extra protection in heavy rain, and more especially high wind.

Always travel as light as possible. I should like to repeat Tom Stephenson's advice: "First pack your rucksack; then empty it on the floor and repack, leaving at home half the things you first thought of."

ALLOW ADEQUATE TIME. If you estimate an average speed of two to two-and-a-half miles an hour, which is slower than most walkers' normal pace, it allows for the time you will spend resting, getting lost, exploring, and being held up by bad weather.

IN AN EMERGENCY be sure of your position on the map. The immediately most obvious descent is not necessarily the safest or best. There is safety in numbers on the hills. With three people, if one is injured, one party can go for help and the third stay with the injured person, who can be sheltered in the lee of a hedge, if he can safely be moved. Bracken and other foliage will help to provide warmth, as will hot tea (not alcohol).

Public transport in the Border

While the Dyke Path is cut in many places by bus routes, the services are invariably geared to the main market centres of Hereford, Shrewsbury, Oswestry and Chester, and rarely provide direct links between places on the Border itself. Careful timetabling and planning will be necessary if you hope to leave your car at the start of a day's walk and return to it at the end by public transport.

Apart from the main tourist areas (the Wye Valley and Vale of Llangollen) services are skeletal; and except for the Abergavenny–Hereford corridor crossed at Pandy, the whole section between Monmouth and Hay is devoid of public transport.

The only places now served by British Rail are Chepstow, Knighton, Welshpool, Chirk and Prestatyn.

The following bus timetables will be useful:

Eastern Area timetable: Gwent, Powys and Royal Forest of Dean. Available from Red and White Services Ltd., The Bulwark, Chepstow, Gwent, or Western Welsh Omnibus Co. Ltd., 253 Cowbridge Road, Cardiff CF5 5XX.

Crosville timetables: Area 1, Area 3 and Area 5. Available from Crosville, Crane Wharf, Chester CH1 3SQ.

Accommodation and Camping

For the most part you should have little difficulty in finding accommodation along the route, from three-star hotels, to private houses and farms; and each year, as the footpath becomes more firmly established, more places well away from the tourist areas are willing to provide a night's lodging for walkers.

The Offa's Dyke Association (address below) publishes a list of places offering accommodation which it regularly updates. Information on where to stay may also be obtained from the Ramblers' Association Bed and Breakfast Guide, the British Tourist Authority (Caravan and Camping Sites and Farmhouse Accommodation in Britain), Wales Tourist Board (accommodation lists).

Since, for many of the farms and private houses, taking in walkers is a sideline you would do well to phone in advance before you set out in the morning, if not before, to be assured of a friendly welcome and a meal when you arrive. The Wye Valley and Black Mountains are popular tourist areas. Many of the places tend to get booked early and you may in the season have to book several weeks in advance. Except during the July Eisteddfod you should find no great difficulty finding somewhere to stay in the Llangollen area.

There are only seven Youth Hostels reasonably near to the Path, and three of those, at Glascwm, Clun and Maeshafn, are an hour or more away on foot. The hostels are open only to members of the Youth Hostels Association. The addresses are:

		Grid ref.
Severn Bridge	Mounton Road, Chepstow, Gwent NP6 6AA	ST 523934
St Briavels	The Castle, St Briavels, Lydney, Glos. GL15 6RG	SO 559045
Capel-y-ffin	King George VI Hostel, Capel-y-ffin, Abergavenny, Gwent NP7 7NP	SO 250328
Glascwm	The School, Glascwm, Llandrindod Wells, Powys LD1 5SE	SO 158532
Clun	St Thomas Close, Clun, Craven Arms, Salop SY7 8JA	SO 304813
Llangollen	Tyndwr Hall, Birch Hill, Llangollen, Clwyd LL20 8AR	SJ 231412
Maeshafn	Holt Hostel, Maeshafn, Mold, Clwyd CH7 5LR	SJ 208617

There are few planned camp sites along the way as yet. A number of farms are prepared to allow casual camping. The Camping Club of Great Britain and Ireland will be able to assist with any enquiries.

Address of the Offa's Dyke Association: Old Primary School, West Street, Knighton, Powys LD7 1EW

Places of interest open to the public

Below is a list of the places of interest in the order in which they occur along the Dyke Path. The opening times of those in the care of the Department of the Environment are indicated as follows:

A   any reasonable time
SM   Sunday mornings from 09.30, April to September
S   Standard hours as follows:

	Weekdays	Sundays
March – April	09.30 – 17.30	14.00 – 17.30
May – September	09.30 – 19.00	14.00 – 19.00
October	09.30 – 17.30	14.00 – 17.30
November – February	09.30 – 16.00	14.00 – 16.00

Closed Christmas Eve, Christmas Day, Boxing Day

	Grid reference	Opening times
Chepstow Castle	535942	S SM
Chepstow Town Walls	53 93	A
Tintern Abbey	533000	S SM
Naval Temple	527124	Accessible at all times
Monmouth Castle	507128	A
Monmouth: Nelson Museum	507129	April, May, June, September, October: 10.30 – 13.00 14.15 – 17.15 July, August: 10.00 – 18.00 Sundays: Easter and Whitsun and in July and August only: 14.30 – 17.30
Skenfrith Castle	457202	A
Grosmont Castle	405244	A

	Grid reference	Opening times
Hen Cwrt	395151	A
White Castle	379167	S
Llanfihangel Court	327203	June and July: first, third and fifth Sundays. August: Sundays. September: first and second Sundays Also Easter, Spring and late Summer Bank Holidays,Sunday and Monday: 14.30 – 18.00
Llanthony Priory	288278	A
Hergest Croft	284566	Open daily, mid-May to mid-June: 11.00 – 19.00
Montgomery Castle	221968	A
Powis Castle	214064	Gardens: 1 May – 30 Sept. Castle: 1 June – 30 Sept. Daily except Monday and Tuesday. 14.30 – 18.00
Old Oswestry	294010	A
Chirk Castle	268381	May – Sept. inclusive: Tuesday, Thursday, Saturday and Sunday: 14.00 – 17.00 only. Also Easter Saturday and Sunday and each Sunday until May: 14.00 – 17.00. Easter Monday, Spring and Summer Bank Holidays: 11.00 – 17.00
Castell Dinas Brân	222431	Accessible at all times
Llangollen: Plas Newydd	218415	Weekdays 09.00 until dusk Summer Sundays only
Valle Crucis Abbey	205441	S SM
Pillar of Eliseg	202445	A
Denbigh Castle	052657	S SM
Rhuddlan Castle	023779	S SM

Early closing days and shopping facilities

C: indicates a choice of shopping facilities, including specialist shops like shoe shops in case your boots give out.

L: indicates a more limited range of shops, mainly for essential provisions. Banking facilities usually available.

In even the smallest hamlet, with very few exceptions, post office facilities are available.

Chepstow	C	Wednesday	Welshpool	C	Thursday
Tintern Parva	L	Thursday	Oswestry	C	Thursday
Monmouth	C	Thursday	Chirk	L	Thursday
Abergavenny	C	Thursday	Llangollen	C	Thursday
Hay-on-Wye	C	Tuesday	Ruthin	C	Thursday
Kington	C	Wednesday	Mold	C	Thursday
Presteigne	L	Thursday	Denbigh	C	Thursday
Knighton	C	Wednesday	St Asaph	C	Thursday
Clun	L	Wednesday	Rhuddlan	C	Thursday
Montgomery	L	Saturday	Prestatyn	C	Thursday

The Country Code

Guard against all risk of fire

Fasten all gates

Keep dogs under proper control

Keep to the paths across farm land

Avoid damaging fences, hedges and walls

Leave no litter

Safeguard water supplies

Protect wild life, wild plants and trees

Go carefully on country roads

Respect the life of the countryside

Select book list

Bingley, Rev. W. *North Wales, Delineated from two Excursions, through all the interesting parts of that highly beautiful and romantic country, and intended as a guide to future tourists.* Longman, Hurst, Rees, Orme and Brown. 2nd edition. 1814.

Beazley, E. and Brett, L. *North Wales.* Faber and Faber. 1971. (A Shell Guide.)

Borrow, G. *Wild Wales.* Everymans Library.

Brecon Beacons: National Park Guide No. 5. H.M.S.O. 1967.

British Regional Geology: The Welsh Borderland. North Wales. Bristol and Gloucester District. H.M.S.O.

Broadley, A.M. *Doctor Johnson and Mrs Thrale: Including Mrs Thrale's unpublished journal of the Welsh Tour made in 1774 and much hitherto unpublished correspondence of the Streatham Coterie.* The Bodley Head. 1910.

Charles, B.G. *Non-Celtic Place Names in Wales.* London Medieval Studies, University College, London. 1938.

Davies, E. (Ed.) *Gazetteer of Welsh Place Names.* University of Wales Press.

Defoe, D. *A Tour through the Whole Island of Great Britain.* Everyman Library. 1962.

Fairs, G.L. *A History of the Hay.* Phillimore and Co., Ltd. 1972.

Fletcher, H.L.V. *Portrait of the Wye Valley.* Robert Hale, London.

Forestry Commission Guide: *Dean Forest and Wye Valley.* H.M.S.O. 1974.

Foster, Ll. and Alcock, L. *Culture and Environment: Essays in Honour of Sir Cyril Fox.* Routledge and Kegan Paul.

Fox, Sir Cyril *Offa's Dyke: A Field Survey of the Western Frontier Works of Mercia in the Seventh and Eighth Centuries A.D.* Oxford University Press. 1955.

Fraser, M. *Welsh Border Country.* Batsford. 1972.

Howse, W.H. *Radnorshire.* E.J. Thurston. 1949.

Jones, G. and Jones, T. (translators) *The Mabinogion.* Everyman's Library. 1949.

Millward, R. and Robinson, A. *The Welsh Marches.* Macmillan. 1971.

Plomer, W. (Ed.) *Kilvert's Diary: Selections from the Diary of the Rev. Francis Kilvert.* Jonathan Cape, London. 1960.

Rees, W. *An Historical Atlas of Wales, from Early to Modern Times.* Faber and Faber. 1972.

Ryder, T.A. *Portrait of Gloucestershire.* Robert Hale, London.

Sylvester, D. *The Rural Landscape of the Welsh Borderland.* Macmillan.

Waite, V. *Shropshire Hill Country.* J.M. Dent and Sons Ltd. 1970.

Badger